Military Sexual Trauma Support Services

Monica J. Rivers

Abstract

The purpose of this qualitative descriptive study was to understand how female military survivors of active-duty military sexual trauma who reside within the United States would describe the effects of their post-military provided mental health care services on their quality of life and well-being. Maslow's Hierarchy of Needs and Deci and Ryan's SelfDetermination Theory were used to understand how the quality of life and well-being of the female veteran participants related to contributing to their basic human needs, selfdetermination, and life fulfillment. The research questions that guided this study were: How do female veterans of MST describe their experiences with mental health care services after discharge? How do female veteran survivors of military sexual trauma describe the effects of post-military mental health care services on their quality of life and well-being? The sample was female veterans who experienced military sexual trauma while on active duty and sought mental health services for their post-active service trauma care in the United States in 2004 or after. The Quality-of-Life survey (QOLS), semistructured individual interviews, and a reflection journal were data sources. Analysis was done using Saldaña's manual coding and Yin's pattern matching. Female veteran survivors of MST experienced a more positive outcome with their QoL and well-being when they received timely mental health care and engaged with a supportive mental health care provider.

Keywords: Military sexual trauma, MST, quality of life, well-being, female veteran mental health care services

Table of Contents

Chapter 1: Introduction to the Study

Introduction

The purpose of this qualitative descriptive study was to understand how female military survivors of active-duty *military sexual trauma* (italicized words and phrases not part of direct quotations are provided in the Definition of Terms and are specific to their use in this study) who reside within the United States would describe the effects of their post-military provided mental health care services on their *quality of life* and well-being (Kelly, 2021; Kintzle et al., 2015; Matt et al., 2020; Reinhardt et al., 2023). Military sexual trauma (MST) describes soldiers, male or female, who experienced "sexual assault or *sexual harassment* during military service" (U.S. Department of Veterans Affairs, 2025). MST has been a problem since at least World War II (Valente & Wight, 2007). Programs and legislation have been enacted over several decades to lower the instances of MST; however, it continues to occur at high rates in females, with approximately 33% of women in the military affected (Preston et al., 2022).

Previous research focused on veterans and *childhood sexual assault* (CSA), suicide risk, and combat exposure (Bosch et al., 2020; Holliday et al., 2023). Matt et al. (2020) found that understanding the type of care most beneficial to the veteran who has experienced MST should be a focus of future research. Although the number of sexual assaults is increasing every year (Gillibrand, 2021a), limited research remains concerning how the services and support provided to these female survivors affect their quality of life and well-being (Kelly, 2021; Kintzle et al., 2015; Matt et al., 2020; Reinhardt et al., 2023). The focus of the study was to highlight female veterans' experiences with services and support specific to MST treatment and their quality of life and well-being post-active duty.

Chapter 1 introduces my study with a discussion of the study's background, definition of terms, anticipated limitations, and summary and organization of the remainder of the study. Chapter 2 will begin with an introduction to the literature review, an expanded review of the study's background, an identification of the problem space and theoretical foundations, a review of the literature, and a problem statement, and concludes with a summary of the chapter. Chapter 3 will cover methodology. It will begin with an introduction, the purpose of the study, research questions, rationale for qualitative methodology, rationale for the research design, population and sample selection, sources of data, trustworthiness, data analysis collection and management, data analysis procedures, ethical considerations, assumptions and delimitations, and ends with a summary of the chapter.

Background of the Study

MST has been a problem in the military since at least World War II (Valente & Wight, 2007). It was and remains a pervasive problem in all military branches with multiple root causes, such as *gender stereotypes,* the historical and religious view of women, the military culture and *hyper-*

masculinity, and myths about sexual assault (Castro et al., 2015; Hahn et al., 2021). With the growing number of women entering and serving within the United States Armed Forces branches, it is crucial to address the problems female service members face relative to MST (Brown et al., 2021). Gillibrand (2022a) reported that the 2021 Department of Defense (DoD) Annual Report on Sexual Assault in the Military cited 8.4% of active-duty women reported unwanted sexual contact within the previous year, showing a rise from previous reporting. On average, one in four women (25%) reported experiencing MST while serving in the military on active duty (Preston et al., 2022). More recently, in the 2023 Fiscal Year Department of Defense Annual Report on Sexual Assault in the Military, 6.8% of active-duty women and 1.3% of active-duty men reported some unwanted sexual contact in the military. The report cited this as a decrease from the last in 2021, the first decrease in about 10 years (U.S. Department of Defense Sexual Assault Prevention and Response Office, 2025). Women are more likely to be sexually assaulted in the military than they are to be shot by an enemy during wartime conflict (Cole et al., 2022).

The military has a long history of sexual assault allegations, such as the 1991 Tailhook Association Convention, 1996's Aberdeen Proving Grounds, military conflicts that occurred during the Gulf War, and the Vanessa Guillen case in April 2020 (Burgess et al., 2013; Pearle et al., 2020). In 2021, Major General William T. Cooley, a United States Air Force commander, was the first General in the Air Force's history to be courtmartialed for sexual assault stemming from a 2018 accusation and was subsequently found guilty in 2022

(Cohen, 2021; Hernandez, 2022). Although many programs and legislation have been proposed, federal lawmakers continue to work toward regulating reporting practices and protecting men and women who serve within the U.S. Armed Forces from MST and their subsequent mental health needs from further sexual assault
(Gillibrand, 2022; U.S. Department of Veterans Affairs MST Fact Sheet, 2021).

MST contributes to adverse mental and physical health outcomes such as increased suicide risk, posttraumatic stress disorder (PTSD), depression, anxiety, chronic pain, obesity, sexual dysfunction, and substance abuse (Kelly, 2021; Preston et al., 2022;
U.S. Department of Veterans Affairs, 2025). Evidence-based practices to treat veterans who experienced MST and their mental health outcomes that arose post-MST included cognitive processing therapy (CPT), prolonged exposure therapy (PE), eye movement desensitization and reprocessing (EMDR) therapy, warrior renew group therapy, and trauma-informed yoga (TIY; Matt et al., 2020; Romaniuk & Loue, 2017; Zaccari et al., 2022). Pharmacologic treatment and the comprehensive care provided through the Veterans Health Administration (VHA) are also treatment routes veterans can utilize (Lee, 2021; Matt et al., 2020).

Prior research focused on veterans and childhood sexual assault (CSA), combat exposure, and suicide risk (Baca et al., 2021; Bosch et al., 2020; Gross et al., 2019; Holliday et al., 2023; Monteith et al., 2019). The research that needs to be better understood is the specific therapy or mental health techniques for sexual trauma victims (Matt et al., 2020; Preston et al., 2022; Starzynski et al., 2017). Researchers have strongly suggested that the mental health care for female veteran survivors of MST and their postmilitary experiences be further studied for their quality of life (QoL) and well-being (Cole et al., 2022; Holland et al., 2016; Kintzle et al., 2015; Reinhardt et al., 2023). This study provided insight and understanding about female veterans who experienced MST while on active duty, their mental health services, and their QoL and well-being as veterans.

Definition of Terms

This study explicitly used the following terms to help the reader understand the meaning and context:

Adverse Childhood Experiences (ACEs). Adverse childhood experiences occur before the age of eighteen years, including, but not limited to, sexual, physical, and emotional abuse, witnessing violence, experiencing family members who have mental or substance abuse problems, and parental separation. These ACEs increase the risk of highrisk situations and or environments (Doucette et al., 2023).

Anhedonia. Anhedonia, often referred to as the opposite of Hedonia, refers to negative thinking and mood and is related to suicidal ideation concerning PTSD MST (Blais & Geiser, 2019).

Childhood Sexual Abuse and Assault (CSA). Childhood sexual abuse and assault is childhood maltreatment that involves the touching, fondling, or sexual touching and intercourse between the ages of birth and 18 years old by an adult person or a person at least five years older than the individual (Holliday et al., 2023). CSA usually occurs within trusted relationships where the perpetrator is depended on for victim safety (Holliday et al., 2023).

Cognitive Processing Therapy (CPT). Cognitive processing therapy is an evidence-based therapy that focuses on cognitive restructuring (Matt et al., 2020; Suris et al., 2013). It is usually a 12-session therapy, but it can vary depending on the patient's response. The goal of CPT is to reduce negative cognitions that veterans have about themselves, other people, and the world around them due to trauma. When these negative cognitions are reduced, psychological improvements are made (Matt et al., 2020).

Descriptive Design. Descriptive design is used to understand who, what, and where the sample population was involved and is organized logically (Lambert & Lambert, 2012). Descriptive design allows a researcher to ask direct questions that elicit thoughtful responses (Maglivy & Thomas, 2009).

Distress. Johnson et al. (2017) described distress as "an unpleasant experience that can affect patients' cognition, behavior, emotion, social well-being, and spirit" (p. 1).

Distress Protocol. Distress protocol involves questions about emotional distress, suicidality, homicidal ideation, and the need for immediate professional attention (Draucker et al., 2009). When researching sensitive topics, Draucker et al. (2009) indicated that these protocols are necessary if the research has the potential to exacerbate emotional distress, such as anxiety, depression, embarrassment, and acute stress reactions.

Eudaimonia. Eudaimonia is a goal of positive psychological health that develops through living up to one's full potential, functioning at one's best level, and understanding one's character (Cooke et al., 2016; Disabato et al., 2016). Eudaimonia can be related to a person's search for the meaning of life (Disabato et al., 2016).

Gender Stereotypes. Gender stereotypes within the military are beliefs that, because of femininity, an individual cannot perform effectively and has a decreased ability to lead others (Brownstone et al., 2018).

Hedonia. Hedonia is the absence of negativity and focuses on a positive sense of life (Cooke et al., 2016). Hedonia also increases pleasure and decreases pain, emphasizing greater emotional states (Disabato et al., 2016).

Homeostasis. Homeostasis is when the body (mechanisms coordinate) maintains a regular bloodstream through the sugar, calcium, protein, oxygen, and water content levels (Maslow, 1943).

Hypermasculinity. Hypermasculinity in the military is a group of patriarchal values that support ideals of aggression, dominance, and competition (Castro et al., 2015). Often, this leads to the trend of feeling threatened by women in power, thus leading to inappropriate verbal and physical contact within the military workplace
(Castro et al., 2015).

Institutional Betrayal. Institutional betrayal refers to an institution that, when charged with protecting a victim, fails to prevent further harm or responds in a way that is not beneficial for the victim (Monteith et al., 2021).

Institutional betrayal may explain why some MST survivors do not report their trauma (Kelly, 2021). These actions can lead to further emotional distress and loss of trust in the institution (i.e., the military; Kelly, 2021; Monteith et al., 2021).

Mental Health Treatment. Mental health treatment pertains to individual therapy, group therapies, and or medication management to treat mental health disorders such as PTSD, depression, and anxiety (Matt et al., 2020; McLean et al., 2022).

Military Sexual Trauma (MST). Military sexual trauma is sexual assault and or sexual harassment experienced by active-duty women or men while serving in activeduty training, inactive training, or otherwise on active duty in any capacity, position, or rank (Monteith et al., 2019; U.S. Department of Veterans Affairs, 2025).

Posttraumatic Growth. Posttraumatic growth refers to the positive psychological differences in a trauma survivor resulting from the individual dealing with and processing their trauma (Reinhardt et al., 2023). Posttraumatic growth can yield a "better appreciation of life and a sense of one's personal strength" (Reinhardt et al., 2023, p. 2).

Posttraumatic Stress Disorder (PTSD). PTSD is a psychiatric disorder that originates from a traumatic event and is characterized by an intense fear from the past trauma that results in exaggerated responses, living in flight or fight mode, and a heightened sense of fear (Brunetti et al., 2017), as well as hypervigilance, avoidance, mood impairment, and hyperarousal (Kelly et al., 2021).

Prolonged Exposure Therapy (PE). PE incorporates breathing exercises, trauma psychoeducation, facing things that have been avoided due to the trauma, and imaginal re-exposure to the trauma (Holder et al., 2020). PE therapy is usually 10-15 sessions, 1-2 times per week, for approximately 90 minutes (Banducci, 2021; Holder et al., 2020).

Qualitative Methodology. Qualitative methodology aims to understand the attitude or experience of participants and how they respond to a particular phenomenon (McCusker & Gunaydin, 2015). The objective is to understand a person's subjective life experiences (Delgado-Hito & Romero-Garcia, 2021).

Quality of Life (QoL). QoL involves an individual's psychological, social, and functional aspects of life (Neugebauer, 2002). QoL can also be used interchangeably with well-being (Cooke et al., 2016). Well-being involves a subjective evaluation of whether an individual feels that their most important needs, goals, and wishes have been achieved (Bullinger & Quitmann, 2022; Frisch et al., 1992).

Sexual Harassment. Behavior occurring in the workplace that is sexual and unwanted by the recipient (Cortina & Areguin, 2021). The behavior is offensive, derogatory, demeaning, humiliating, and perceived as threatening an individual's wellbeing (Cortina & Areguin, 2021).

Suicidal Ideation. Suicidal ideation is the thought of being better off dead or hurting oneself somehow (Blais et al., 2023).

Trauma-Informed Yoga (TIY). Trauma-informed yoga is a form of therapy that uses mindfulness, breathing techniques, relaxation, and physical activity to improve feelings of safety, empowerment, collaboration, and trustworthiness (Braun et al., 2021).

Warrior Renew Therapy. Warrior renew therapy focuses on the experiences veterans have had through betrayal, injustice, and lack of closure (Matt et al., 2020). The usual Warrior Renew treatment is a 12-week protocol with 24, 2-hour sessions. The Warrior Renew group therapy is based on Epstein's cognitive-experiential therapy, which proposed two different systems of processing information: the rational and the experiential (Epstein, 2003; Katz & Jensen, 2022).

Anticipated Limitations

Anticipated limitations are identified as weaknesses or problems within a study for which the researcher has little or no control (Ellis & Levy, 2009; Theofanidis &

Fountouki, 2018). Limitations can influence research findings (Price & Murnan, 2004). Anticipated limitations are essential within a study because they allow readers to be wellinformed and to make decisions based on the information presented (Greener, 2018). The following are examples of limitations for this study:

- Limitations of data sources.
    - Self-reported data. Participants in this study self-reported their experiences and their outcomes without a way to verify their information (Ross & Bibler Zaidi, 2019).
    - Levels of service received. Due to the timing of this study, study participants are post-active-duty female veterans who have received varying levels of services and were at different stages of well-being. The population and sample were limited by the stage of well-being and quality of life (QoL; Reinhardt et al., 2023).

  - Geographic location. This study's geographic location included female veterans living within the United States of America at the time of their participation. Because of the small sample size, this study’s findings cannot be generalized to other global locations, female veterans of other nations, or female veterans of the United States Military and its branches (Taherdoost, 2022; Theofanidis & Fountouki, 2018).

- Limitations of sampling strategy.
  - Purposive sampling. Purposive sampling is when candidates are recruited to be included in the study because they meet the qualifying criteria and are willing to share their information; potential for bias may be present (Etikan et al., 2016).
  - Snowball sampling. Snowball sampling is known to have a high potential error rate because recruitment is based solely on referrals from participants already involved in the study (Bhardwaj, 2019).
  - Convenience sampling. Convenience sampling is the least reliable sampling strategy because these sources are usually not the most informative but are easily accessible (Staller, 2021). Transferability is poor in convenience sampling because this strategy presents high sampling error (Bhardwaj, 2019).

Summary and Organization of the Remainder of the Study

Chapter 1 introduced this study's purpose and helped establish the need to understand the topic further. This study aimed to assist in providing information to complement published research about military sexual trauma and to fill gaps in those studies. This study was guided by Maslow’s hierarchy of needs and self-determination theory.

Chapter 2 identifies the problem space (i.e., gap), the theoretical foundations, an exhaustive review of extant and current literature, and the study’s problem statement, and concludes with a summary of the chapter. Chapter 3 continues with the purpose of the study, research questions, rationale for qualitative methodology, the research design, population and sample selection, data sources, trustworthiness, data collection and management, data analysis procedures, ethical considerations, and assumptions and limitations. The chapter will conclude with a summary of Chapter 3. Chapter 4 will begin with an introduction and continue preparing raw data for analysis, descriptive data, data analysis procedures, and results, concluding with a summary. Chapter 5 will include a study summary, findings and conclusions, implications, and recommendations.

Table 1

Alignment Table

Alignment Item	Alignment Item Description
Problem Space Need:	Researchers have strongly suggested that the mental health care for military female sexual trauma survivors and their post-military experiences be further studied for Quality of Life (QoL) effects (Cole et al., 2022; Holland et al., 2016; Kintzle et al., 2015; Reinhardt et al., 2023).
Problem Statement:	It was not known how female military survivors of active-duty military sexual trauma would describe the effects of their post-military provided mental health care services on their quality of life and well-being (Kelly, 2021; Kintzle et al., 2015; Matt et al., 2020; Reinhardt et al., 2023)
Purpose of the Study:	The purpose of this qualitative descriptive study was to understand how female military survivors of active-duty military sexual trauma who reside within the United States would describe the effects of their post-military provided mental health care services on their *quality of life* and well-being.
Phenomenon:	The phenomenon that was studied is how the mental health services received after MST have contributed to the female veterans' perceptions of QoL and well-being after discharge from the military.
Research Questions:	R1) How do female veteran survivors of military sexual trauma describe their experiences with mental health care services after discharge? R2) How do female veteran survivors of military sexual trauma describe the effects of post-military mental health care services on their quality of life and well-being?
Methodology/Research Design:	Qualitative descriptive

Chapter 2: Review

Introduction to the Chapter and Background to the Problem

The purpose of this qualitative descriptive study was to understand how female military survivors of active-duty military sexual trauma (MST) who reside within the United States would describe the effects of their post-military provided mental health care services on their quality of life and well-being (Kelly, 2021; Kintzle et al., 2015; Matt et al., 2020; Reinhardt et al., 2023). Researchers have strongly suggested that mental health care for military female sexual trauma survivors and their post-military experiences be further studied for quality of life (QoL) effects (Cole et al., 2022; Holland et al., 2016). MST continues to grow within the military, and the need for services and resources to contribute to a female veteran's QoL and well-being grows in importance

(Gross et al., 2019; McKenzie et al., 2021; Stirman et al., 2021; Williams et al., 2017).

Chapter 2 will provide a background of the problem, theoretical foundations, and literature review. Chapter 2 continued with the problem statement, a summary of the chapter, and the groundwork for the study. Major and recurring themes from seminal and current MST research, well-being, QoL, and their individual and aggregate connection to MST survivors' post-military separation are discussed.

The information used for this literature review was primarily obtained through the

Grand Canyon University online library and, to a lesser extent, Google Scholar, and EBSCO. The key search terms used were MST, military sexual assault (MSA), QoL, selfdetermination theory, Maslow's hierarchy of needs, self-determination theory, and wellbeing. Further, the following keywords were used to identify scholarly studies on female veterans: rape, wellness, trauma, eudaimonia, anhedonia, and hedonia.

The information presented within this chapter will summarize the relevant literature and explain the need for additional research based on identifying the problem space suggested in the extant literature. Previous studies focused on active-duty women in the military and women veterans who experienced MST and how their experience related to suicidal ideation and or attempted suicide, their exposure to combat, and or their history of childhood sexual assault (CSA; Baca et al., 2021; Bosch et al., 2020; Gross et al., 2019; Holliday et al., 2023; Monteith et al., 2019). Previous studies did not specifically focus on how female veterans with a history of MST perceived the effect(s) of military mental health services they received while on active duty, their post-activeduty mental health services, and how those services may or may not have contributed to their well-being and quality of life post-military service (Reinhardt et al., 2023).

This chapter is organized and begins with an Introduction and background of the study. It then continues with the identification of the problem space, theoretical foundations, a review of the literature, and the problem statement. Finally, it ends with a summary of all sections.

Identification of the Problem Space

It was not known how female military survivors of active-duty military sexual trauma would describe the effects of their post-military provided mental health care services on their quality of life and well-being (Brown et al., 2021; Calhoun et al., 2018; Holland et al., 2016; Kintzle et al., 2015; Matt et al., 2020; Starzynski et al., 2017). MST has been acknowledged as an issue within the military since World War II (Valente & Wight, 2007; Wolff & Mills, 2016). However, in the past decade, MST has gained exposure, and survivors have gained support, including Congressional investigation and proposed legislation that addresses MST during and post active duty (Gillibrand, 2022b). The exposure has allowed for the addition of policies, services, and programs to aid in justice for the survivors and work toward their healing as the Veterans Health Administration (VHA) increases its focus on a whole health model considering physical, mental, emotional, and spiritual health and well-being (Pebole et al., 2021).

Although MST has increased, there continues to be limited research that examines how mental health services contribute to the female veteran QoL and well-being after assault (Kelly, 2021; Kintzle et al., 2015; Matt et al., 2020; Reinhardt et al., 2023) while serving on active duty and during life as a veteran. Researchers have strongly suggested that military mental health care for female sexual trauma survivors and their experiences post-military be further studied for its lifespan QoL effects (Cole et al., 2022; Holland et al., 2016; Kintzle et al., 2015; Reinhardt et al., 2023). Matt et al. (2020)

suggested that future research focus on determining which facet of care offers the most benefit to veteran survivors of MST. QoL and well-being have received scant research on female veteran populations regarding the services and support they have received after an activeduty assault.

Monteith et al. (2019) examined 108 veterans who reported a history of MST to identify suicidal ideation, attempts, and the factors associated with post-suicide and postsuicidal ideation. Seventy-five percent of the study's veteran population reported suicidal ideations, and 40.7% reported suicide attempts. The authors concluded that addressing posttraumatic self-beliefs may be necessary in managing the risk for suicidal ideations and attempts. In a secondary analysis with a sample of 126 women with PTSD, Bosch et al. (2020) presented a way to determine how cognitive processing therapy (CPT) for PTSD treatment in women who have experienced childhood sexual trauma affects their QoL. Bosh et al. concluded that while CPT helped to reduce PTSD symptoms, it did not necessarily increase QoL in survivors of sexual trauma. Gross et al. (2019) completed a study utilizing 330 female veterans to explain further the correlation between military sexual assault (MSA), combat exposure, and PTSD. Gross et al. concluded that combat exposure and MSA were strong predictors of PTSD. Although the research from Bosch et al. and Gross et al. provided important information about female veteran survivors of MSA and MST, the female veteran survivors' perceptions of increased QoL and wellbeing after mental health services rendered were not the focus of the research.

Holliday et al. (2023) created a data analysis to examine the link between CSA and MST as factors that increase suicidal ideation and suicide attempts. The findings found a strong correlation between CSA, MST, and suicidal ideation and attempts. The authors concluded that although the VA offered MST access, the understanding of veterans' access was limited. The study supported the importance of screening veterans throughout their lifetime for MST and being able to link them to the appropriate services to fit their needs, even as their needs change.

Holland et al. (2016) research goal was to identify how the barriers to helpseeking after MST for men and women veterans affected their well-being. The authors explained the need to eliminate barriers for veterans seeking help following MST. Their study was a secondary analysis of data initially collected by the United States Department of Defense (DoD) in 2010. The men and women veterans in that study were found to have higher PTSD symptoms and the presence of greater help-seeking barriers.
"Assessing experiences of sexual assault and help-seeking behaviors across the entirety
of employees' military career would further explicate the impact of experiences and barriers on psychosocial wellbeing" (Holland et al., 2016, p. 258). Kintzle et al. (2015) also found that future research should be focused on how interventions delivered after the trauma are related to reducing the long-term effects of MST over the survivor's lifetime. Kelly (2021) posited that women attributed their treatment-seeking barriers to the military culture and enlisted experiences. These women felt the military was "a man's world"

and decided against seeking treatment. Kelly's (2021) research supported the common theme that women in the military continue to feel that there are barriers to seeking help for the trauma they experienced, and studies needed to focus on care delivered to reduce trauma symptoms.

This study intended to address what was not known about the utilization of mental health services in their contribution to the QoL and well-being of female veteran MST survivors and what aspects of mental health services they reported led to increased QoL and well-being. Holland et al. (2016) discovered that if help-seeking barriers were present after MST, an increase in PTSD was present within the affected population. Bosch et al. (2020) suggested that female veterans with a history of CSA were likelier to have had a history of poor QoL. Holliday et al. (2023) added that the same population was at risk for increased suicidal ideation. Monteith et al. (2019) found that managing suicide risk after MST began with the survivor addressing their negative posttraumatic beliefs. Gross et al.
(2019) supported the previous findings of Holland et al., Bosch et al., and Monteith et al. that MST interacted with combat exposure to increase the likelihood of PTSD and explained that those findings supported the continued need for prevention and treatment of MSA to improve well-being.
Addressing this problem can increase access to mental health care with more favorable treatment outcomes for our female veterans and activeduty members (Kimerling, 2017).

Doucette et al. (2023) suggested prescreening of enlistees for sexual trauma and other adverse childhood experiences (ACEs) before entering the military. Individuals who have previously experienced sexual assault are more likely to also experience revictimization as an adult, such as MST, while in the military (Holliday et al., 2023). This approach would help to provide direct support and prevention throughout the enlistee's military career, thus laying the groundwork for more healthy outcomes. Materials and programs to educate the providers administering care to these veterans are essential to meet their needs better (Burgess et al., 2013).

Stander and Thomsen (2016) suggested that the military evaluate the success of its prevention and response efforts focused on the most critical components for success. In 2013, Senator Gillibrand, the chair of the Senate Armed Services Personnel Subcommittee, introduced the Military Justice Improvement Act (MJIA) to change how reports of military sexual assault were handled (Gillibrand, 2020). Under this new legislation (Senate Bill 1520), the chain of command would no longer handle complaints, and the legal processes followed under the Uniform Code of Military Justice (UCMJ). It was introduced to Congress yearly from 2014 until 2020 but never passed (Gillibrand, 2022b). In 2021, Senator Gillibrand changed portions of the bill, held press conferences and hearings, and attached it as an amendment to the National Defense Authorization Act (NDAA). Finally, in June 2022, it was passed as the Military Justice Improvement and Increasing Prevention Act (MJIIPA) under NDAA. (Gillibrand, 2022).

Theoretical Foundations

Maslow's hierarchy of needs theory (1943) and Deci and Ryan's (1985a) selfdetermination theory (SDT) were used to understand the phenomenon of military sexual trauma therapy services post-military service. These theories focus on fulfilling needs based on a hierarchy to obtain self-determination and a positive quality of life (Deci et al., 1994; Ventegodt et al., 2003). The theories are presented as theories of human motivation and determination from positive psychology to explain the human drive for higher satisfaction (Deci & Ryan, 2000; Maslow, 1943). Female veteran military sexual trauma (MST) survivors who have actively engaged with mental health services and have had or have not had an experience that has contributed to their lifespan QoL were the focus of this study.

Maslow's Hierarchy of Needs

In Maslow's (1943) motivational theory, he suggested that survival needs and the need to feel safe were the basis of fulfillment before any other human need could be met (N. Parker, 2021). Maslow's hierarchy of needs described how individuals develop their full potential (Sirgy, 1986). Maslow also explained that when an individual completed one level of satisfaction and potential, they would move onto the next level, eventually arriving at the highest level, self-actualization and or intrinsic values. Extreme stress or trauma inhibits individuals from identifying and satisfying their needs, making it difficult to move through the stages of Maslow's hierarchy of needs (N. Parker, 2021).

Maslow's original theory (1943) was based on five basic needs: physiological, safety, belonging, esteem, and self-actualization (see Figure 1). Before Maslow's death, he added a sixth need, intrinsic values, and acknowledged that other needs were not initially included in his early publications (Skelsey-Guest, 2014). Tripathi (2018) and Maslow described physiological needs (e.g., breathing, food, water, sex, sleep, clothing, shelter, homeostasis, and excretion) as the foundations of life's basic needs. Tripathi described safety needs as security, protection, stability, and freedom from fear. The authors included love and belonging as the third need, encompassing friendship, intimacy, trust, giving and receiving affection, and belonging. Next in the hierarchy are esteem needs, which include independence, self-respect, respect from others, and status. Self-actualization was and remains the fifth and highest of Maslow's original hierarchy of needs. Maslow defined self-actualization as working to reach one's potential and striving for identity or self-growth (Tripathi, 2018). Self-actualization relates to motivation and relates well to Deci and Ryan's (1985b) self-determination theory.

Figure 1

Author Depiction of Maslow's Hierarchy of Needs Model

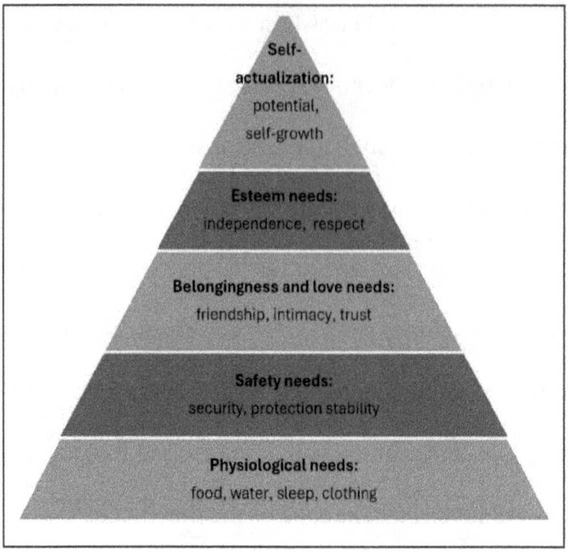

Self-Determination Theory (SDT)

Deci and Ryan (1985a) developed the self-determination theory to describe motivation and identify resilience as having a positive effect on well-being and quality of life (QoL; Perlman et al., 2018). Perlman et al. explained that one's level of selfdetermination was regulated by the level of support within the areas of autonomy, competence, and relatedness. The authors further explained that the more support received within these areas, the higher the level of motivation, resulting in higher levels of self-determination. Within SDT, autonomy develops when individuals can act independently but use their volition to rely on others (Deci & Ryan, 2006). These higher levels of self-determination then contribute to increased QoL and well-being. Perlman et al. (2018) found that 106 participants with mental health diagnoses, such as schizophrenia, depression, schizoaffective disorder, anxiety disorder, and personality disorder, validated Deci and Ryan's theory.

The results indicated that the level of support was related to self-determination and resilience.

SDT bases a person's motivation upon their personality traits, self-motivation, and the external conditions that positively encourage these processes (Ryan & Deci, 2000). Motivation is often viewed as autonomous or intrinsic, but it can also drive external factors related to an individual's culture or extrinsic motivation (Ryan & Deci, 2020). Ryan and Deci explained that intrinsic motivation involves exercising personal capacity and seeking challenges to learn and explore new things for personal satisfaction. Extrinsic motivation does the opposite; it relies upon performance based on something other than personal satisfaction, possibly compliance (Ryan & Deci, 2000). The authors, Ryan and Deci (2000), concluded that whether the motivation is intrinsic or extrinsic, the trauma survivor engaged in treatment will be positively affected.

Trauma and Theory

Trauma survivors must actively participate in their healing process to reach their highest potential once their basic survival and psychological safety needs have been met (N. Parker, 2021). The author further explained that self-care behaviors were difficult for trauma survivors and that barriers to self-determination must be considered.

Hypervigilant behaviors and chronic issues often are prevalent when trauma creates stress that inhibits the individual's readiness to learn (N. Parker, 2021). According to the Readiness to Learn Self-Care Model for Trauma Survivors, clinicians must understand how trauma survivor clients learn and their readiness to learn because these are essential factors in the contribution of their autonomy and recovery (N. Parker, 2021).

Maslow's hierarchy of needs and understanding the effects of the female veteran services and support received after MST on their quality of life and well-being go hand in hand. As discussed, Maslow's hierarchy of needs suggested that survival needs and the need to feel safe were the basis of fulfillment before any other human needs could be met (N. Parker, 2021). Sexual assault undermines fulfilling these basic needs and makes it difficult to progress within the hierarchy. PTSD is one of the many results of MST, and Zuch (2015) explained that PTSD is a barrier to physical and mental wellness that can force an individual into a lower level of self-actualization, making progress difficult.

Self-determination theory focuses on progress through motivation (Perlman et al., 2018). In applying this theory, MST services and support that strive to provide for basic human needs (i.e., autonomy, competence, and relatedness to others) are foundational to motivation and well-being (Mancini, 2008). If the treatment setting in which female veterans receive treatment is supportive, it will greatly affect motivation and well-being outcomes (Mancini, 2008). Therefore, locating and engaging in competent services and support is important to achieving well-being and quality of life.

Review of the Literature

The purpose of this qualitative descriptive study was to understand how female military survivors of active-duty military sexual trauma (MST) who reside within the United States will describe the effects of their post-military provided mental health care services on their quality of life and well-being (Kelly, 2021; Kintzle et al., 2015; Matt et al., 2020; Reinhardt et al., 2023). This section serves as the framework for the body of literature relating to the phenomenon of Military Sexual Trauma (MST), some of the services and support provided in response to MST effects, and how the services and support provided relate to well-being and quality of life (QoL). The review is structured into background information, therapies and pharmacologic treatment, well-being, and QoL. Each section is broken into sub-topics to understand the scope of the problem and the purpose of my study. Finally, the problem statement is restated, followed by a summary of Chapter 2.

Military Sexual Trauma Background Information

The U.S. Department of Veterans Affairs (VA; 2025) has defined military sexual trauma (MST) as "sexual assault or repeated, threatening sexual harassment experienced during military service" (para.1). Military service is serving on active duty within any of the six military branches (i.e., Army, Navy, Coast Guard, Marine Corps, Airforce, and Space Force) and or their Reserve National Guard components. MST can affect all military members, not just one group or branch.

Sexual assaults rose 5% yearly from 2006-2012, and a 53% increase in reports from 2012-2013 (Hickey et al., 2017). Even though women make up less of the military population than men, women are about nine times at greater risk of experiencing military sexual trauma (MST; Morral & Schell, 2021). Morral and Schell (2021) shared that the 2018 Workplace and Gender Relations Survey of Active-Duty Members reported that 6.2% of women were sexually assaulted in 2020. Morral and Schell suggested that it was also important to mention that service members who did not identify as heterosexual also had an increased rate of sexual assault.

According to Lee (2021), the Annual Report on Sexual Assault for Military Fiscal Year 2018 released by the Department of Defense (DoD) reported an increase in MST from the report the previous year by at least 10%. The report indicated a higher MST rate in the Navy and the Marines, higher within enlisted personnel than officers, and for female veterans than male veterans. The U.S. Department of Defense Sexual Assault Prevention and Response Office (2023), in its Annual Report on Sexual Assault for Military Fiscal Year 2021, indicated that 8.4 % of women service members and 1.5% of men service members experienced unwanted sexual contact in the prior year. The report also cited 8,866 reports of unwanted sexual contact, an increase of 1,050 reports from the fiscal year 2020. Barth et al. (2016) explained that MST is also higher for deployed women than non-deployed women. The report indicated that more military members are coming forward in their reporting, showing increased reports over the years (Ferdinando, 2018). The author explained that an average of 1 in 3 members chose to report their assault, up from about 1 in 14 in 2006. MST has an extensive history within the military that continues to occur (Acierno et al., 2021; U.S. Department of Defense Sexual Assault Prevention and Response Office, 2025). MST affected military soldiers from World War II to Operation Iraqi Freedom and Operation Enduring Freedom, producing many mental health symptoms and concerns that could last a lifetime (Lee, 2021).

Early Military Sexual Trauma. Historically, women served an ancillary role in the military until they were integrated in 1979 with their male counterparts (Wolff & Mills, 2016). Finally, in 2013, the ban was lifted, restricting women from being on the front lines in direct combat (Calhoun et al., 2018). Valente and Wight (2007) suggested that sexual assault and sexual trauma within the military had existed since at least World War II (WWII). The authors further wrote that during WWII, military sexual assault (MSA) and MST were not discussed nor reported by its service members. During the Vietnam veteran era (1955-1975), the interest in MSA and MST increased, and this was when the first reports of MST were recorded (Lee, 2021). Conard et al. (2016) reported that approximately 4% of female service members reported MST during the Vietnam era and reported accounts of being called derogatory names and being blamed for their assault by their military peers upon their return to a duty station after deployment.

Vietnam veteran-era female veterans began reporting decreased quality of life (QoL) due to increased PTSD, depression, and alcohol use disorders because of the MST they endured and the response that they received (Conard et al., 2016). Valente and Wight (2007) found that no discussion about possible actions for the attacker or counseling for the survivors was part of the military mental healthcare for the few women who reported a sexual assault during that time. There was a lack of military review after the attack, and counseling services were minimal until the Persian Gulf War (1990-1991) when there was an increase in female veterans reporting their incidents (Valente &

Wight, 2007).

Tailhook Association Convention. There have been several incidents of sexual misconduct and or assault within the military that made media headlines involving female soldiers and their male counterparts. Valente and Wight (2007) recounted several sexual assault allegations within the U.S. Military, such as the 1991 Tailhook Association Convention (Tailhook) in Las Vegas that involved female Naval officers. The female officers were lined up, groped, and had some clothing removed by intoxicated, highranking male Naval senior and junior officers. Conard et al. (2014) explained that Tailhook was a point in the history of sexual assault allegations when the discussion about MST was the most active. The authors further explained that Tailhook helped provide a more fully defined definition of MST and increased acknowledgment and recognition of MST.

Public Law 102.585 was initiated after Tailhook and began legislating laws and guidelines that would later be applied to processing, prosecuting, and treating assailants and survivors (Mead, 2019). In 1992, a Congressional mandate, The Veterans Health

Care Act of 1992, was introduced; it mandated Veterans Affairs to treat distress related to MST (Burgess et al., 2013; Romaniuk & Loue, 2017). Directly following this mandate, the authors shared that 61% of Veterans Affairs medical centers had developed treatment teams to treat sexual assault within the military. Yet, there continued to be several other accounts of MST and still a long road toward prevention and treatment.

Aberdeen Proving Grounds. In 1996, at the US Army's Aberdeen Proving Ground (Aberdeen), assault charges were brought against male officers by their female trainees (Burgess et al., 2013). Cerretti (2016) explained that in that incident, there were several trainers engaged in improper "relationships," as defined by military regulations with trainees, which included "abuse of power, death threats, harassment, and rape" (p. 803). These relationships were often known as fraternization in the military and are punishable under Uniform Code of Military Justice (UCMJ) Article 134 (U.S. Department of Defense Sexual Assault Prevention and Response Office, 2023). Cerretti wrote that during the investigation into the Aberdeen assaults, a designated telephone hotline number was established so the female trainees could file complaints. Ceretti also wrote that thousands of calls were received within the first week of the designated hotline, leading to further investigations and additional charges against Army trainers other than those initially charged.

In 2000, the Veterans Health Administration finally mandated soldiers to be universally screened for MST throughout all VHA facilities under the Veterans

Millennium Health Care Act (Burgess et al., 2013; Romaniuk & Loue, 2017). In 2004, Secretary of Defense Donald Rumsfeld initiated an investigative task force into the current reporting and prevention policies used within the military and made recommendations for change and improvement (Burgess et al., 2013). That task force found 35 factors that influenced the processing and reporting of MST and provided nine actions for correction and improvement (Burgess et al., 2013).

Other MST. Adding to the previously named occurrences were reported incidents of rape in Kuwait during the Gulf War and in Haiti, Okinawa, and Kosovo during the early 1990s while the US military occupied those areas, respectively. In 2003, the U.S. Air Force Academy was identified as ignoring sexual assault from 1993-2002, with more than 50 cases reported (Burgess et al., 2013). The incidents of rape and sexual assault within the military continued from 2010-2011 when four male instructors were charged with sexual encounters and rape with female trainees at Lackland Air Force Base in Texas, a basic military training site. Wolff and Mills (2016) researched female veterans who served from 1979 to the early 2000s and found that women who joined the military upon integration (1979-1992) reported the highest level of MST. The authors revealed that many participants had experienced more than one form of MST during their enlistment.

Vanessa Guillen. MST continues to occur within today's military (2025). Pearle et al. (2020) found that MST gained public attention in the case of Vanessa Guillen, an Army soldier from Fort Hood, TX. In April 2020, Vanessa vanished from the Army base and was later found murdered by a fellow male soldier who had been sexually assaulting her (Pearle et al., 2020). She was murdered in an armament storage room after she decided to report the sexual assault. Reports indicated that a civilian committee investigated Fort Hood in general after the Guillen murder and determined that it had an accepting culture of MSA and MST (Thayer, 2021). Following the investigation, it was reported that several individuals within the chain of command were relieved of their duty for their lack of leadership, and the base commander was returned from a deployment to initiate a training program (Thayer, 2021).

Military Sexual Trauma Reporting. Gross et al. (2019) reported that an estimated 20-43% of women veterans were survivors of military sexual trauma (MST).

Burgess et al. (2013) reported that one in five women and one in 500 men experienced some form of MST while serving in the military. It was difficult to have an accurate report due to the lack of reporting that occurred because of the sufferer's loss of confidence in the military system or their fear of backlash (Monteith et al., 2016). Caplan (2013) described being sexually assaulted by a fellow unit member as like being assaulted by a family member due to the closeness of the relationships and bonds built within a unit. According to betrayal trauma theory, developed by Freyd in 1996, posits that survival accounts for a victim's dissociation from their trauma (DePrince & Freyd, 2002), and betrayal blindness occurs when the survivor and witnesses of the trauma feel reluctance in reporting because the perpetrator is someone they trusted within a trusted environment or system (Andersen & Blais, 2019; Monteith et al., 2022; Sivers et al., 2002). It is an innate protective factor due to the human response of wanting to preserve an environment, relationship, or social system (Andersen & Blais, 2019). Within the military environment, the survivor must continue to rely upon a system that has not protected them and often must work beside their perpetrator. *Institutional betrayal* is associated with trauma-related anxiety, dissociation, and sexual difficulties (Monteith et al., 2021). It can greatly increase symptoms of depression, PTSD, and thoughts or attempts at suicide (Monteith et al., 2022). Institutional betrayal may explain why some MST survivors do not report their trauma (Kelly, 2021). These actions can lead to further emotional distress and loss of trust in the institution (i.e., the military; Kelly, 2021; Monteith et al., 2021).

Caplan (2013) explained that sometimes receiving care from military and nonmilitary therapists can also be traumatizing as some therapists may suppress or minimize the trauma presented. The veteran may avoid therapy to avoid being diagnosed with a mental health condition, which will follow them throughout their military career and potentially affect their ongoing promotions or obtain specific military clearances. Sometimes, not disclosing the trauma feels easier and aids in avoiding guilt and shame about the trauma (Lee, 2021).

Blais et al. (2018) conducted a study with 359 female veterans to understand better the rate of MST reported, the rate of nondisclosure during the MST screening process, the factors that influence nondisclosure rates, and how veterans described their barriers to disclosing MST during screening. The results indicated that 143 of these veterans reported a history of MST, while 35 reported they had not disclosed their MST status during screening. A higher nondisclosure rate was reported when the assailant was a fellow unit member. Of the 35 who did not disclose, some indicated nondisclosure due to stigma factors, feeling unsafe to report, or not being screened promptly. The authors concluded that there was reason to believe that MST rates were higher than Veteran's Affairs estimates. The authors suggested that efforts needed to be made to ensure veterans felt supported and safe when reporting MST so that the disclosure rate would represent the actual rate of traumas.

Currently, the military has provided a two-tiered system, restricted and unrestricted reporting, for MST created by the Department of Defense (DoD) under the Sexual Assault Prevention and Response (SAPR) Policy (U.S. Department of Defense Sexual Assault Prevention and Response Office, 2023, para. 2). A restricted report is for a survivor who wants medical and mental health treatment for MST but who would not want to disclose other information about the trauma. With this type of restricted report, the perpetrator is not held accountable for his or her actions (Burgess et al., 2013). An unrestricted report would allow the survivor to seek medical and mental health treatment and would also mean that the survivor seeks punishment for their assailant and would have to engage in the proceedings (Burgess et al., 2013; Conard et al., 2014; GonzalezPrats, 2017). Before this more structured way of reporting was introduced, soldiers would have to report the assault to their unit commanders, who possessed the power to decide whether the report should be taken any further (Gonzalez-Prats, 2017). The author pointed out this was flawed because the commanding officers lacked the training and expertise to investigate and ascertain whether a crime had been committed. It was unfair and could pose a conflict of interest if the perpetrator had a personal or professional relationship with the commanding officer; thus, a change had to be made in 2013 to provide more structure to the reporting (Gonzalez-Prats, 2017).

Andersen and Blais (2019) reported that an estimated 38% of female service members reported MST due to barriers in reporting. The authors explained that many reported survivors were encouraged to "drop the issue" (p. 373) or did not reach a resolution after reporting. The authors concluded that retaliation was a serious concern when reporting MST or MSA. Farris et al. (2021) reported that in 2014, 30% of female military members who experienced sexual assault also experienced retaliation. With reporting, the individual feared scrutiny from others or being labeled a traitor (Caplan, 2013).

Farris et al. (2021) researched factors that increased retaliation. The authors obtained information to understand whether the survivor disclosed the trauma to no one, a trusted confidant, a friend or family member, or a mandatory reporter. Retaliation measures were measured as no retaliation, social retaliation, and or professional retaliation. Also, information about the type of assault was collected. Results indicated that female survivors who filed unrestricted reports or disclosed the trauma to a mandatory reporter received considerably higher retaliation than other female survivors.

This group was also more likely to receive professional retaliation than the other groups.

The authors concluded this was due to investigations initiated from an unrestricted report. Social retaliation often came from someone of a higher rank than the survivor. Greater psychiatric problems and revictimization were associated with sexual assault nondisclosure (Blais et al., 2018; Calhoun et al., 2018) and negative responses after reporting a negative effect on well-being (Mercado et al., 2015). When veterans experienced negative responses to their reporting, they encountered institutional betrayal, increasing the risk of veteran suicide (Matt et al., 2020). Often, these veterans disclosed that an insufficient response to a sexual trauma report felt just as distressing as the initial trauma (Lofgreen, 2020).

MST Outcomes. MST contributes to poor physical and mental health outcomes. Survivors of MST may experience PTSD, depression, anxiety, suicidal ideation, suicide attempts, substance abuse, and several other associated adverse mental health outcomes (Kelly, 2021; Preston et al., 2022; U.S. Department of Veterans Affairs, 2023). Blais et al. (2017) found that veterans with a history of MST were two times more likely to develop eating disorders than veterans who did not have a history of MST. Mankowski and Everett (2016) explained that there was a 59% risk for mental health problems when someone encountered MST. Medical conditions such as liver and pulmonary disease, hypertension, obesity, STDs, HIV, and endometriosis were also prevalent within the MST population of veterans (Burgess et al., 2013). Due to physical and mental health disorders, female veterans with a history of MST often suffered from a poorer QoL when compared with female veterans who had never been assaulted (Burgess et al., 2013). It is important for practitioners who are not VA Healthcare providers to know and understand how to identify their veteran population, ask the necessary questions to determine whether MST is a factor, and know how to treat the veteran effectively (Lee, 2021).

The Sexual Assault Task Force was created in 2004 by Secretary of Defense Donald Rumsfeld after sexual assault allegations were made by service members deployed to Iraq and Kuwait (Gonzalez-Prats, 2017). The task force was implemented to identify ways to eradicate military sexual assault (Gonzalez-Prats, 2017). The task force team suggested a more structured reporting system with improvements in support for the victims (U.S. Department of Defense Sexual Assault Prevention and Response Office, 2023). In October 2004, in response to the task force's suggestion, the Sexual Assault Prevention and Response Office (SAPRO) was formed (Gonzalez-Prats, 2017). The SAPRO continues to be responsible for implementing guidelines for all military branches in their prevention and response training (Gonzalez-Prats, 2017; Lofgreen, 2020). Each military branch must submit an annual report to Congress regarding military sexual assaults (Hickey et al., 2017). Since the implementation of the SAPRO, an increase in sexual assaults within the military has been reported (Preston et al., 2022).

A female veteran MST survivor and her history of childhood sexual assault, suicide attempts or suicidal ideation, and deployment are the focus of several recent studies (Baca et al., 2021; Bosch et al., 2020; Gross et al., 2019; Holliday et al., 2023; Monteith et al., 2019). However, those studies did not focus on the female veteran and their experience with MST services and their perception of how their specific support may or may not have contributed to an increase in their well-being and QoL.

Understanding how female veteran survivors describe the services and support received is essential to move forward in the treatment and care programs for female active duty and veterans (Matt et al., 2020).

Military Sexual Trauma Therapies and Pharmacologic Treatments

Services and Support. Women veterans in the United States who have experienced MST have unique healthcare needs. With these veterans' prevalent mental and physical health complications, it is crucial to address existing healthcare disparities (Kehle-Forbes et al., 2017). To provide effective MST care and support, survivors must first complete screening. Conard et al. (2016) explained the importance of asking specific questions when screening to determine the types of services and support that can and need to be offered to female veterans. "Have you ever served in the military?" is an essential first question that can open many doors of opportunities for healing in these female veteran MST survivors (Conard et al., 2016). Follow-up questions recommended by the National Center for Posttraumatic Stress Disorder and the Walter Reed Army Medical Center included "While you were in the military, did you experience any unwanted sexual attention, such as verbal remarks, touching, or pressure for sexual favors?" and "Did anyone ever use force or threat of force to have sex with you against your will?" (Romaniuk & Loue, 2017, p. 86). Services and support for survivors of MST are important for the healing process. Services and support can come as individual, group, or medication management therapies, also known as psychotropic treatment (Matt et al., 2020). Also, holistic healing as a complementary modality, such as yoga and meditation, has been found helpful in the healing process (Braun et al., 2021; Matt et al., 2020). Incorporating a comprehensive model of care would aid in reducing symptoms associated with MST (Matt et al., 2020). Voelkel et al. (2015) pointed out that although MST was clearly defined, few studies have explored the effectiveness of treatments offered to the veteran population for trauma (Matt et al., 2020).

Although services and support are available to survivors of MST, not all female veterans seek treatment (Andersen & Blais, 2019). The authors explained that self-stigma was a large part of this barrier. Self-stigma involves negative beliefs about admitting to a mental illness and seeking treatment for that illness (Andersen & Blais, 2019). The authors explained that self-stigma also involves fear that the survivor will be discriminated against once others learn about their treatment or diagnosis. Goffman's theory of stigma explains that because of the stigma attached to mental health, victims are inclined to conceal their condition deliberately, so they are not seen as less of a person or as being tainted (Andersen & Blais, 2019). Blais et al. (2018) completed a study examining MST nondisclosure. Of the 289 participants, 143 of them reported MST screening, and 35 of those reported nondisclosure of MST, where half of them attributed their nondisclosure to stigma.

Evidence-Based Practices (EBP). The VA supports evidence-based practices in treating post-traumatic stress disorder (PTSD) due to MST, which targets mental health symptoms such as anxiety, avoidance, and negative beliefs (Katz, 2016). Some EBPs that VHA supports are cognitive processing therapy (CPT), prolonged exposure (PE) therapy, eye movement desensitization and reprocessing (EMDR) therapy, warrior renew therapy, skills training in affective and interpersonal regulation (STAIR), stress inoculation therapy (SIT), trauma-informed yoga (TIY), and dialectical behavioral therapy (DBT;

Hundt et al., 2020; Romaniuk & Loue, 2017). For my study, only CPT, PE, EMDR,

Warrior Renew, and trauma-informed yoga therapies will be addressed.

Cognitive Processing Therapy (CPT). Cognitive processing therapy (CPT) is an evidence-based therapy that focuses on cognitive restructuring (Matt et al., 2020; Suris et al., 2013). CPT was initially developed by Resick and Schnicke in 1993 to treat civilians who were sexual assault survivors (Mead, 2019). It was further developed and is now accepted and effective in treating PTSD in veterans with MST and is the only treatment validated for veterans diagnosed with PTSD due to MST (Holder et al., 2019). CPT is usually provided for twelve sessions that are 50 minutes long. This exposure-based therapy is effective in reducing PTSD and challenging beliefs and interpretations that assist survivors in overcoming their traumatic experiences (Galovski et al., 2022; Zappert & Westrup, 2008). The goal is to reduce negative cognitions that veterans have about themselves, other people, and the world around them, and when these negative cognitions are reduced, psychological improvements are made (Matt et al., 2020).

Holliday et al. (2017) studied how the therapeutic response to CPT affects Black and White female veterans of MST-related PTSD. The participants were recruited from large Southwestern VA Medical Centers through posted advertisements, recruitment letters, and referrals from clinicians who conducted the recruitment. Out of the initial 161 female veterans enrolled in the study, only 109 were randomly used, resulting in 52 female veterans being included in the CPT study. Many participants were excluded due to the incompetence of one CPT therapist; of those 52, 16 identified as White and 20 as Black. Informed consent was given before participants were given the ClinicianAdministered PTSD Scale (CAPS), the PTSD Checklist (PCL), and a socio-demographic questionnaire. The CAPS measures re-experiencing, avoidance and numbing, and arousal symptoms associated with PTSD from MST.

Participants were provided 12 one-hour weekly or bi-weekly CPT sessions by trained therapists to complete the study. Once the studies were completed, the CAPS and PCL were readministered to the participants at the 1-week post, 2, 4, and 6-month postCPT sessions. The therapeutic results varied in the post-test but not when comparing Black and White female veterans. PCL scores showed improvement from baseline to 1week post-treatment but no differences in racial self-identification. Re-experiencing symptoms improved from baseline to 1 week and one week to 6 months post-treatment, but again, there was no difference in racial self-identification. Avoidance numbing symptoms showed improvement from baseline to 1-

week post-treatment only with no significant differences with racial self-identification.

Arousal symptoms showed improvement from baseline to 1-week post-treatment, and again, no significant differences with racial self-identification. The study showed no differences in sessions attended by Black and White female veterans and no differences in early termination. The authors concluded that CPT was tolerated well and effectively among Black and White female veterans. The authors further suggested that future research should continue to monitor whether CPT treatment improves PTSD-related symptoms over a more extended period. The authors mentioned an increased therapeutic response and adherence when Black patients were matched with Black therapists. Their study provided evidence that CPT was an effective intervention for Black and White veterans with MST-related PTSD.

Prolonged Exposure Therapy (PE). Prolonged Exposure (PE) therapy is a trauma-focused treatment based on emotional processing therapy (Banducci, 2021). PE therapy incorporates breathing exercises, trauma psychoeducation, facing things previously avoided due to the trauma, and imaginal re-exposure to the trauma (Holder et al., 2020). PE therapy is usually 10-15 sessions, 1-2 times per week, for approximately 90 minutes each session (Banducci, 2021; Holder et al., 2020). Usually, sessions consist of four parts: psychoeducation, breathing retraining, exposure to trauma-related signals, and imaginal exposure (Romaniuk & Loue, 2017). Individuals receiving this type of therapy must be watched closely due to the challenging extent of the treatment. It is important to evaluate the individual often, as treatment should be stopped if it is not showing effectiveness to the patient (Holder et al., 2020). If effective, the veteran experiences more confidence in managing distress symptoms (Matt et al., 2020). Dropout rates contribute to the ineffectiveness of PE. Avoidance of exposure to reexperiencing the traumatic event due to emotion dysregulation is the main reason for dropout among women veterans with MST (Gilmore et al., 2020). Attrition leads to untreated PTSD, which continues to affect veterans' lives and provides occupational, relationship, and societal consequences (Hundt et al., 2020). PE therapy has recently been determined to be an effective treatment used via telehealth (Banducci, 2021).

Holder et al. (2020) conducted a study to determine the median effective dose of PE therapy needed for veterans with PTSD. Holder defined the median effective dose in the study as the number of sessions needed for a clinically meaningful improvement from a veteran's baseline. Veterans were recruited who had been diagnosed with postdeployment PTSD (p. 2). Holder studied 10,234 veterans who received PE as a part of VHA care from 2001 to 2017. The authors determined that four sessions were the mean effective dose that provided clinically meaningful improvement in their PTSD symptoms. Although completing all treatment sessions to work toward symptom remission would be necessary, four sessions provided some symptom changes. Holder et al. (2020) provided evidence that PE is an effective therapy in treating veterans with PTSD, accounting for low attrition and completion of the program.

Previous studies have found that Cognitive Processing Therapy (CPT) was effective in reducing PTSD symptoms in veterans with MST history and found that CPT and PE therapy, when used together, constituted the most effective treatment therapy (Khan et al., 2020; Schnurr et al., 2022; Suris et al., 2013; Voelkel et al., 2015). Khan et al. (2020) concluded that the impact of CPT and PE treatment for PTSD and MST differed in male and female veteran survivors. The authors found no significant difference in responses in the posttraumatic checklists by gender before treatment was given, and there was a mutual decrease in symptoms present for both males and females post-treatment. Holder et al. (2019) posited that CPT is the ideal treatment for reducing PTSD symptoms, although Schnurr et al.'s (2022) research trial comparing CPT and PE could not determine whether CPT or PE offered the most benefit to veterans with PTSD.

Eye Movement Desensitization and Reprocessing (EMDR) Therapy. EMDR was introduced by Shapiro in 1989, and studies and research trials with veterans continue to grow (Shapiro, 2002). EMDR was designed to assist with decreasing symptoms of PTSD, specifically in the areas of nightmares, flashbacks, and heightened arousal (Cole et al., 2022). It was offered in eight phases and worked to alter the maladaptive responses that individuals had with the memories of (Schwarz et al., 2020); the eight phases are history taking, preparation, assessment, desensitization, installation, body scan, closing, and referral (Hurley, 2015). Schwarz et al. (2020) explained that EMDR was found to require fewer sessions with the greatest symptom reduction in veterans with combatrelated PTSD; there have not been many that focused on veterans specifically with MST.

Schwarz et al. (2020) conducted a study involving 21 women with a history of sexual or domestic violence. They were provided eight sessions of EMDR. Progress was measured quantitatively through participants' completion of mental health scales and measures (anxiety, depression, trauma, and distress) and qualitatively through researcher journaling activities following interviews. Once treatment concluded, participants reported decreased depression, anxiety, and PTSD symptoms and enhanced confidence and hope. The study supported previous research that EMDR was an effective approach to trauma treatment.

Warrior Renew (Group) Therapy. Warrior renew therapy was explicitly developed for veterans with MST histories and focuses on the experiences these veterans have had through betrayal, injustice, and lack of closure (Matt et al., 2020). The usual Warrior Renew treatment is a 12-week protocol with 24 two-hour sessions. Warrior Renew group therapy is based on Epstein's cognitive-experiential therapy, which proposes two different systems of processing information: the rational and the experiential (Katz & Jensen, 2022). The authors explained that the rational system processes things that are considered facts and that could be considered logical and analytical. The experiential system is the opposite and is based on emotions, imagery, and associations, which cannot be generalized. This type of experiential therapy within warrior renew group therapy sought to build trust, safety, and a feeling of a shared community to begin working on psychoeducation and interpersonal issues (Katz, 2016; Katz & Jensen, 2022).

Katz and Sawyer (2020) conducted a trial study for the warrior renew group therapy. The purpose was to determine whether a brief treatment effectively reduced anxiety, posttraumatic symptoms, negative cognitions, and depression in female veterans. The authors used 8 weeks with 8, two-hour sessions and found that brief group therapy was an acceptable route of treating symptoms secondary to MST with a reduction in most posttraumatic negative cognitions. Katz and Jensen (2022) evaluated a 5-day workshop based on the Warrior Renew program to determine whether it effectively reduced anxiety, depression, and negative cognitions within the female veteran population. Eighteen female veterans participated in the pre- and post-study surveys, which indicated a positive response. The authors found that their symptoms had significantly decreased through the interventions provided at the workshop. Warrior Renew therapy has provided evidence that either a traditional or hybrid program provided significant symptom relief in female veterans with MST history.

Trauma-Informed Yoga (TIY). Braun et al. (2021) indicated that complementary and integrative health modalities were growing in interest within the VHA and Department of Defense (DoD) as a treatment modality for veterans with a history of MST. Veterans have expressed an interest in treatment that is not psychotherapy or psychopharmacologic (Zaccari et al., 2022). Trauma-informed yoga was recommended for women trauma survivors due to its therapeutic qualities and effective affect regulation

(Braun et al., 2021). The authors found that this therapy used mindfulness, breathing techniques, relaxation, and physical activity to improve feelings of safety, empowerment, collaboration, and trustworthiness.

Braun et al. (2021) studied seven female survivors of MST to explore the effectiveness of TIY in reducing MST symptoms, including, but not limited to, depression, PTSD, physical symptoms, and other psychosocial stressors. Of the seven participants, two left the study. The five remaining veterans had a history of MST, served in various military branches, and were enrolled in mental health treatment within the community at the time of the study. They reported MST experiences from sexual harassment to rape, while others reported child sexual assault (CSA) and adult sexual assault outside the military. In the study, the veterans were enrolled in mindful yoga therapy and attended classes once weekly for 75 minutes each over 12 weeks. After completion, most veterans reported reduced stress, PTSD symptoms, depressive symptoms, and improved mood, sleep, mindfulness, and relaxation. The authors suggested further studies to research TIY's true impact on veteran women with a reported history of MST. Although further studies were suggested, the authors provided evidence that TIY was an effective treatment for veterans with symptoms related to MST.

Pharmacologic Treatment/Medication Therapies. Veterans presenting with symptoms of PTSD and other disorders have the option of receiving psychotherapy and or pharmacologic interventions (Matt et al., 2020). Selective serotonin reuptake inhibitors (SSRIs) and selective norepinephrine reuptake inhibitors (SNRIs) have been the most effective pharmacological treatments for veterans with MST histories (Lee, 2021). Matt et al. (2020) indicated that the U.S Food and Drug Administration (USDA) approved paroxetine and sertraline as a treatment for PTSD to reduce mood and anxiety; benzodiazepines were not recommended due to their high potential for addiction (Lee, 2021). Matt et al. (2020) concluded that other pharmacologic treatments could be prescribed if other physical comorbidities developed.

Figure 2

Services and Support for MST

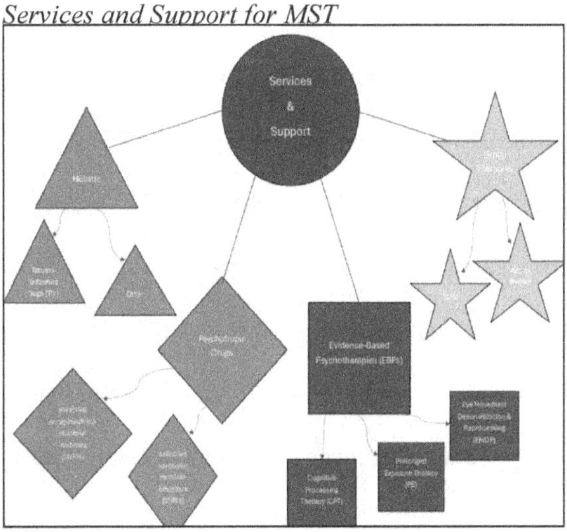

Veterans' Health Administration (VHA) Care. The VHA implemented a universal screening program for MST for new veterans exiting the military or beginning VHA services (Hargrave et al., 2022). If the veteran screened positive for MST, all related care was provided at no charge (Calhoun et al., 2018; Kelly et al., 2021). Universal screening was new in 2002 and fully implemented in 2004 as a permanent benefit under Public Law

108-422 (Calhoun et al., 2018; Kelly et al., 2021). VA providers are encouraged to ask all patients about MST directly; each VA Healthcare facility has a liaison who coordinates care and ensures changes are made to ensure appropriate care for MST survivors (Hickey et al., 2017). In 2010, VHA began mandating gender-sensitive care for women to provide access to mental health, gynecology, and physical health care (Kehle-Forbes et al., 2017).

Outreach is important in informing eligible and non-eligible veterans about the care and resources available through the VHA healthcare system (Calhoun et al., 2018). It is also important for healthcare providers to understand MST and be sensitive to the mental and physical health problems that it contributes to (Barth et al., 2016). Monteith et al. (2021) suggested that clinicians working with veterans and military members should assess a soldier's perception of institutional betrayal, as this may affect the treatment engagement with VHA services. Calhoun et al. (2018) suggested that further research to understand better the differences in veterans with an MST history who do and do not utilize VHA care was important to understand. Follow-up was critical to ensuring the well-being of these female veterans who are obtaining supportive care (Conard et al., 2014). Kehle-Forbes et al. (2017), in their study of 37 female veterans whose history was Vietnam and post-Vietnam era service, who received VA disability for PTSD, and who were with and without a history of MST and VHA care, concluded that female veterans thought the VA was lacking in services for women. The female veterans, specifically those with a history of

MST, felt that the VA lacked sensitivity and fell short of providing care for women and that males were provided the care they felt the VA lacked. Some suggestions for improvement include women-only waiting rooms, increased programs for women, expanding mental health services for women, and expanding VA Health facilities to be more welcoming for children accompanying their parent(s). Overall, the lack of gender-specific care was at the forefront. The authors suggested further studies should be directed at women veterans who use VHA care and those who opt not to use

VHA care.

Military Sexual Assault Services and Well-Being

Deci and Ryan (2006) posited that well-being was thought of as experiences of hedonia and eudaimonia. The authors offered that well-being was the optimal psychological experience and functioning. These two factors apply to how one experiences well-being and how individuals set their lives and motivations to the different things they engage with (Mise & Busseri, 2020). Rahmani et al. (2018) explained that well-being refers to how individuals respond to things they have experienced or would like to have experienced. The authors explained that well-being was challenging to measure and had no concrete definition because any definition would be subjective because it would be a self-evaluation. Well-being is rooted in goals a person has for their life and whether they can achieve them (Mise & Busseri, 2020), with emotion regulation playing a large part in well-being (Ortner et al., 2018). Mise and Busseri (2020) further explained that hedonia and eudaimonia together supported achieving the highest level of well-being with positive life outcomes, which drove the activities that individuals chose to engage in.

Factors such as MST can make it more challenging to achieve well-being during military service and after discharge (Hendrikx et al., 2021). Adjusting from military to civilian life is a difficult process, and with approximately 200,000 service members making this transition each year, it is crucial to understand that some of them will struggle to adapt to life post-military (Vogt et al., 2021). Vogt et al. explained that while post-military well-being is difficult to achieve, it becomes more difficult when other risk factors are considered, such as gender, age, and or rank during separation, pre-military experiences, military experiences, health conditions, and coping mechanisms. The authors found that veterans with a history of MST and or MSA were at greater risk for decreased well-being and poorer outcomes after separating from military service. Ultimately, veterans with a higher support rate and psychological resilience tend to have positive outcomes post-military.

Disabato et al. (2016) attempted to determine how hedonia and eudaimonia represented distinct types of well-being: subjective and psychological. Hedonia was measured as satisfaction with life, happiness, and depression, while eudaimonia was measured as psychological well-being and meaning in life. Well-being was associated with happiness orientations, hope, gratitude, curiosity, grit, search for meaning, rumination, and loneliness. The authors found that aspects of eudaimonia seemed more intentional than those of hedonia, and the motivations related to eudaimonia were more connected to the principles of well-being. The authors stated that measuring well-being in terms of character strength, the meaning of life, and authenticity, instead of being based solely on concepts of hedonia and eudaimonia, were more effective.

Hedonia and Anhedonia. Hedonia is centered around increased pleasure, immediate sensory pleasure, and decreased pain (Disabato et al., 2016; Rahmani et al., 2018). It encompasses how one finds enjoyment or satisfaction in life and is considered subjective well-being (Mise & Busseri, 2020). Mise and Busseri further explained that hedonia was measured on three different factors: self-appraisal of how satisfied they are with their life, possessing a positive effect, and the absence of an adverse effect. Hedonia is the emotions and mood that are felt at the time as an immediate reaction to how people think and feel about their current lives (Jayawickreme et al., 2012). The authors explained that the hedonic approach takes the narrow view, coined by Parfit in 1984, that pleasure is the only positive experience and pain is the only negative experience. An individual with a hedonic focus would seek pleasure and enjoyment regularly (Mise & Busseri, 2020). Conversely, anhedonia refers to negative mood and thinking (Blais & Geiser, 2019). It is directly related to PTSD MST and suicidal ideation (Blais & Geiser, 2019).

Eudaimonia. Eudaimonia is centered around growth and flourishing as a human while living up to one's full potential in self-growth and self-actualization (Disabato et al., 2016; Rahmani et al., 2018). It encompasses positive functioning and finding meaning in one's life. It is focused on relationships, personal growth, self-acceptance, and factors related to meaning and self-reflection (Mise & Busseri, 2020). Someone who is focused on eudaimonic well-being would be an individual who seeks meaningful and authentic life experiences that would contribute to their personal growth (Mise & Busseri, 2020).

Military Sexual Trauma Services and Quality of Life (QoL)

MST survivors are likelier to experience diminished QoL (Williams et al., 2017). As defined by the World Health Organization (WHO), QoL encompasses physical and psychological health, social relationships and relationship to the environment, and level of independence (Cooke et al., 2016). It measures whether one feels their life has been fulfilled (Frisch et al., 1992). Matt et al. (2020) found the importance of understanding how the female veteran experiences this aspect of life after treatment for MST to determine the effectiveness of the treatment (Matt et al., 2020). Providing validating services and support to survivors is beneficial in decreasing mental health symptoms and improving one's QoL (Preston et al., 2022).

Schou-Bredal et al. (2022) conducted a study to explore how sexual assault influences the quality of life, amongst other factors such as health and self-efficacy. The study included men and women in the general Norwegian population; it was not specific to military sexual trauma or assault and was not conducted in the United States.

Participants were provided with checklists and scales to indicate their levels of PTSD, QoL, mental health problems, physical health problems, and self-efficacy. The study complemented previous studies that concluded that sexual assault might reduce an individual's perception of QoL and self-efficacy. The participants also reported worse mental and physical health concerning a lower perception of QoL. Experiencing sexual assault increases other problems and burdens in life; therefore, treatment could help to improve one's QoL and or well-being (Schou-Bredal et al., 2022).

Problem Statement

It was not known how female military survivors of active-duty military sexual trauma would describe the effects of their post-military provided mental health care services on their quality of life and well-being. Holland et al. (2016) and Kintzle et al. (2015) strongly suggested that more research was necessary to understand the mental health services needed for female military veterans who experienced MST while on active duty. Researchers have strongly suggested that mental health care for female military sexual trauma survivors and their post-military experiences be further studied for quality of life (QoL) lifespan effects (Cole et al., 2022; Holland et al., 2016; Kintzle et al., 2015; Reinhardt et al., 2023) because mental health services received after assault did not highlight these outcomes. The extant literature failed to illuminate female veterans MST survivors' perceptions of their experiences with mental health care services in their contribution to their QoL. This study sought to understand the experiences of MST female veteran survivors, how they perceive their experiences with their mental health care as veterans, and how MST and post-service mental health care have affected their quality of life and well-being.

The relevant literature focused on suicidal ideation and attempts following military sexual treatment (MST) in male and female veterans (Monteith et al., 2019), women who experienced childhood sexual trauma (Bosch et al., 2020), and military sexual assault (MSA) in veterans who have been exposed to combat (Gross et al., 2019). As reported by Monteith et al. (2019), Bosch et al. (2020), and Gross et al. (2019), previous literature demonstrated a lack of focus placed on the MST survivor experiences that contributed to increased QoL within the female veteran MST survivor. The history of female veterans' utilization of VA Healthcare services has been limited due to their views about the lack of gender-sensitive care available (Kintzle et al., 2015). The authors found those perceptions led to feelings of being let down by a system that was felt to be designed to treat them.

The population of interest was all military veterans who had experienced military sexual trauma. The target population of interest was female veterans who experienced MST while on active duty and have sought mental health services for trauma care. Although MST has been present in the military for decades, the focus and sample of this study were female veterans who have served since 2004, as this year marks the creation of the SAPR Program, which was established with the goal of MST prevention and treatment (U.S. Department of Defense Sexual Assault Prevention and Response Office, 2023). The goal was to learn from these veterans about the impact of the care they received on their QoL and well-being and the effect that care continues to have on their lives. Information was collected from these female veterans through individual interviews, reflection journals, and a questionnaire. The interviews and reflection journals included 12 female veteran MST survivors who have utilized mental health services. The questionnaires were provided to 20 participants altogether, who also had the option to participate in the individual interviews.

Summary

This chapter summarized the key points and background of military sexual trauma. The groundwork included themes related to the services and support used to treat veterans with MST. Therapies such as cognitive processing therapy (CPT), prolonged exposure therapy (PE), Eye Movement Desensitization and Reprocessing (EMDR)

Warrior Renew therapy, trauma-informed yoga (TIY), and pharmacologic treatment (Banducci, 2021; Brown et al., 2021; Lee, 2021; Matt et al., 2020) were discussed as well as services and support provided through the Veteran's Health Administration (VHA). Maslow's hierarchy of needs (1943) and Deci and Ryan's (1985a) self-determination theory were applied to my study. The theories supported the research questions to better understand how female veterans described the mental health services provided and how that care affected their post-military quality of life (QoL).

Researchers have strongly suggested that the mental health care for military, female sexual trauma survivors and their post-military experiences be further studied for

QoL effects (Cole et al., 2022; Holland et al., 2016; Kintzle et al., 2015; Reinhardt et al., 2023). The extant literature had not examined how female military survivors of sexual trauma described their post-military assault-provided military health care. Much of the previous research focused on childhood sexual assault (CSA), suicide risk, and combat exposure (Baca et al., 2021; Bosch et al., 2020; Gross et al., 2019; Holliday et al., 2023; Monteith et al., 2019). This study focused on female veterans' experiences and how they were and are affected by those experiences. Chapter 3 will introduce the methodology and design, the purpose, the research questions, the population and sample, the trustworthiness, the research data sources, and a final summary of Chapter 3.

Chapter 3: Methodology

Introduction

It was not known how female military survivors of active-duty military sexual trauma would describe the effects of their post-military provided mental health care on their quality of life (QoL) and well-being (Brown et al., 2021; Calhoun et al., 2018; Holland et al., 2016; Kintzle et al., 2015; Matt et al., 2020; Starzynski et al., 2017). Previous research about female veteran survivors of military sexual trauma focused on how it related to childhood sexual assault (CSA), suicide risk, and combat exposure (Baca et al., 2021; Bosch et al., 2020; Gross et al., 2019; Holliday et al., 2023; Monteith et al., 2019). Researchers have strongly suggested that military mental health care for female survivors of sexual trauma and their experiences post-military be further studied for its effects throughout their lifespan (Cole et al., 2022; Holland et al., 2016; Kintzle et al., 2015; Reinhardt et al., 2023). Matt et al. (2020) suggested that future research focus on the facets of care that benefit veteran survivors of MST. QoL and well-being have not been well explored within the female veteran populations as they (QoL and well-being) relate to what services female veterans receive after sexual trauma as a veteran. This research addressed this gap by applying Maslow's hierarchy of needs theory (1943) and Deci and Ryan's (1985a) self-determination theory (SDT). Chapter 3 will provide a detailed review of the study's purpose, research questions, methodology and design rationale, and population and sample selection. It will continue with a discussion of the sources of data for this study, as well as trustworthiness, data collection and management, data analysis procedures, and ethical considerations. The last section will present a summary of the chapter.

Purpose of the Study

The purpose of this qualitative descriptive study was to understand how female military survivors of active-duty military sexual trauma who reside within the United States would describe the effects of their post-military provided mental health care services on their quality of life and well-being. Holland et al. (2016) and Kintzle et al. (2015) strongly suggested that more research was necessary to understand the mental health services needed for female military veterans who experienced MST while on active duty. Mental health services were considered as medication management, psychopharmacology, and cognitive behavioral therapies (CBT). Cognitive behavioral therapies are evidence-based therapies that the VA uses to treat PTSD, the most common diagnosis following MST (Galovski et al., 2022). The phenomenon that was studied was how the effects of mental health care services received after MST by female veterans who have previously served on active duty have contributed to their perceptions of QoL and well-being as veterans.

QoL includes integrating well-being (hedonic and eudaimonic) and wellness (Cooke et al., 2016). Hedonic well-being focuses on life satisfaction, while eudaimonic well-being focuses on positive- psychological health and fulfillment (Cooke et al., 2016; Disabato et al., 2016; Jia et al., 2021). Although not clearly defined due to its broad definition and similarities to eudaimonia, wellness can be measured by the level of functioning that maximizes one's potential (Cooke et al., 2016). With the number of MST reports having risen steadily every year since 2006 and continuing through 2018 (Hickey et al., 2017; Murray et al., 2022), this research study provided information where it is needed to support female veterans who are survivors of MST. Due to the lack of information about the post-assault mental health care services provided by the VHA and other resources and their effective contribution to their QoL and well-being, the effectiveness of these treatments is unknown.

The questionnaires and individual interviews (see Appendix G and H) helped to understand the various services and support within mental healthcare services that female veteran survivors of MST attributed to impacting their quality of life and well-being. The participants were recruited through online veterans' groups and veterans' services, using purposive (Plan A), snowball (Plan B), and convenience (Plan C) sampling. This study recruitment simultaneously utilized Plan A-C to add to the study's feasibility relevant to resources after permission was granted by the gatekeepers, who are responsible for each online group contacted. Research data was collected through an online questionnaire (see Appendix G), individual interviews (see Appendix H), and reflection journals (see Appendix M).

The data collected was manually analyzed first. Coding then continued using Yin pattern-matching (Yin, 2009) and the Saldaña (2009) method (see Appendix J for codebook entry). The findings are presented in Chapter 4.

Phenomenon and Research Questions

The research questions presented helped to elicit and understand the experiences of female veterans who have survived military sexual trauma. The questions focused on how the participants described their experiences with the treatment, services, and resources they were able to utilize as MST survivors after their discharge from the military. Research has found that MST is associated with adverse mental and physical health outcomes (Kelly et al., 2021; Monteith et al., 2020). The responses from the questionnaires and interviews have been used to understand the research questions and have added to the importance of understanding what services and support are beneficial for MST veterans from their experiences.

This study aimed to understand how the effects of mental health services received after active-duty sexual trauma have contributed to female veterans' perceptions of quality of life and well-being after discharge from the military. These veterans' mental health services included individual therapy and group therapy as a primary source of treatment. Mental health services also included classes, psychiatric medications, or any combination of these services.

The following research questions guided the qualitative study:

RQ1: How do female veteran survivors of military sexual trauma describe their experiences with mental health care services after discharge?

RQ2: How do female veteran survivors of military sexual trauma describe the effects of post-military mental health care services on their quality of life and well-being?

Research question 1 contributed to identifying and understanding the unique ways female veteran survivors of MST have utilized military and non-military-provided mental health services. The female veterans who agreed to participate in this study described individual therapy, group therapy, and or psychopharmacology services. The literature suggests that MST survivors will likely experience diminished QoL and benefit from psychotherapy and similar services (Williams et al., 2017).

Research question 2 identified how the services and support received (from research question 1) have influenced participants' well-being and QoL. The literature suggested that different forms of therapy, specifically military resources and medication management are just a few available modalities to treat MST in female veterans (Bosch et al., 2020; Matt et al., 2020). Factors such as sensitivity in treating veterans when seeking help are essential in improving treatment outcomes (Gross et al., 2019; Kimerling et al., 2011).

Primary data made essential contributions to my study. Primary data was obtained directly from a participant, and secondary data was obtained from sources such as published studies and reports (Hox & Boeije, 2005). Questionnaires, individual interviews, and reflection journals comprised the data sources for this research. I acknowledged that while gender is self-identified, the Informed Consent qualification is for "females." The reasoning is that differences between birth sex and identified gender may be outside the scope of the research questions and may not accurately represent females who have experienced MST. Completed interviews, questionnaires, and reflection journals served as primary data.

Purposive (Plan A), snowball (Plan B), and convenience (Plan C) sampling were done to provide a more expansive range of participants from diverse backgrounds. Interview sessions were audio recorded to provide a transcript for thematic analyses. Due to the sensitive nature of my research, *distress protocol(s)* were initiated when participants displayed or expressed emotional distress (Draucker et al., 2009).

Rationale for a Qualitative Methodology

A qualitative methodology was chosen for this research. It was deemed most appropriate for the study because it helps explain a phenomenon and the participants' beliefs, feelings, and thoughts (Delgado-Hito & Romero-Garcia, 2021). Qualitative research aims to understand a participant's subjective experiences relative to the research questions (Delgado-Hito & Romero-Garcia, 2021; McCusker & Gunaydin, 2015). Personal viewpoints and opinions are crucial in generating words and ideas in place of or adding to numerical data to analyze collected data (McCusker & Gunaydin, 2015). Qualitative research uncovers themes and trends in the thoughts and opinions of the groups involved in a study derived from a participant's natural conditions (Park & Park, 2016).

Qualitative methodology involves participants in personal interactions such as focus groups, interviews, observations, and case studies (Yates & Leggett, 2016). The goal is to understand a presented phenomenon in which a similar group's personal experiences and perceptions have been utilized (Delgado-Hito & Romero-Garcia, 2021; Isaacs, 2014). The reliable and valid results come directly from obtaining a complete picture of the information being investigated (Park & Park, 2016). Participants share their stories and points of view, followed by coding and analyses to obtain themes (Delgado-Hito & Romero-Garcia, 2021).

Qualitative methods were utilized within many MST studies to understand experiences and obtain information from male and female veterans (Hundt et al., 2020; Katz & Jensen, 2022; McKenzie et al., 2021). McKenzie et al. (2021) used a qualitative methodology to understand resiliency and posttraumatic growth following sexual trauma in women veterans of the Iraq and Afghanistan wars. The authors found that a woman's desire to connect with other women with similar experiences and be involved in therapy groups was integral to understanding how MST survivors experienced decreased PTSD symptoms and increased QoL. A qualitative methodology was most appropriate for this research study because the purpose was to understand the utilization of a similar group of individuals. It required obtaining more personal data from each participant individually. Most important to this methodology is to gather information from each participant in its most actual form, ensuring that there is little or no deviation from their truth. Because it was not known how female military survivors of sexual trauma while in the military would describe their post-military assault-provided mental healthcare, a qualitative methodology aided in an exploration of their life experiences.

Quantitative methodology was inappropriate for this study because the goal is not to quantify survey data (McCusker & Gunaydin, 2015) but to understand the participants' beliefs, feelings, and or thoughts about the subject. Quantitative research focuses on a "how much" or "how many" question within a study with pre-selected variables (Sandelowski, 2000). For example, Gilmore et al. (2020), using a quantitative methodology, found the phenomenon in their study revealed a significant percentage of women veterans (50%) had dropped out of Prolonged Exposure Therapy (PE) PTSD treatment because of a deficit of emotion regulation. Their goal was to provide numerical data to support their hypothesis. In contrast, this research study aimed to understand the effects of post-assault mental health care services by digging deeper into the beliefs, feelings, and thoughts of female veteran survivors of MST. While numerical data and relationships between presented variables are essential parts of quantitative methodology, qualitative methodology relies on person-to-person interviews or focus groups to develop themes that lead to conclusions for the sample interviewed (Yates & Leggett, 2016). In this study, the individual perceptions of each participant provided the thought processing and application that comprised the statistical calculations.

Mixed methods also were not appropriate for this study. Mixed methods research uses qualitative and quantitative data to analyze a given study's narrative and numerical information (Ostlund et al., 2011). Also, a mixed methods study was not found financially feasible for my research. The participants, female veterans, were able to explain the services and support they received and their outcomes as those outcomes related to their quality of life and well-being, and this was a financially feasible method to address the research questions.

Rationale for Research Design

A descriptive design was utilized for this study. Lambert and Lambert (2012) explained that a descriptive design provides experiences in "everyday terms" by the participants (p. 255). The focus of this study was to understand female veteran survivors' reflections on how their utilization of mental health services contributed to their QoL and well-being relative to Maslow's hierarchy of needs theory (1943) and Deci and Ryan's self-determination theory (1985a); a descriptive design fit the need. Descriptive designs are used to understand events in terms of who was involved, what was involved, where things were involved, from the individual who has lived within that experience, and then are organized logically (Lambert & Lambert, 2012; West et al., 2017). Descriptive design allows a researcher to ask direct questions that elicit more thoughtful responses (Maglivy & Thomas, 2009). West et al. (2017) utilized a qualitative descriptive design to inquire whether trauma-informed yoga was an impactful therapy for participants' PTSD. West et al.'s research questions focused on whether the participants felt any changes in their symptoms after treatment and, if so, how the program impacted their symptoms. The research justified the study's use of a descriptive design because, similarly, the research sought to understand the impact of services and support received on symptoms. The authors found it essential to understand their participants' insights as those who lived through the experiences. Another essential aspect of the descriptive design is allowing participants to share freely without boundaries as part of the open-ended questions (Maglivy & Thomas, 2009).

Phenomenology was not chosen because, while the research and open-ended interview questions require the "lived" experience, the commonality in their emotional and physical reactions questions the uniqueness of each experience. The uniqueness is due to the military protocol, disciplines, and pressure not to disclose MST.

Phenomenology seeks to describe the phenomena between persons instead of allowing for uniqueness in their personal experiences (Neubauer et al., 2019).

The case study design was not chosen because the research questions involve multiple participant experiences to understand the commonalities among veteran survivors of MST. A case study is better suited for a study that seeks to explore, describe, or explain a phenomenon with a single or series of cases and address a "how" or "why" question (Yates & Leggett, 2016). The exploration, description, and explanation of phenomena within a case study are focused on an event, a program, or an activity from one individual (Yates & Leggett, 2016). While the case study design was a probable choice for this study, it does not emphasize free-flowing, everyday terms that are the focus of a descriptive case study with several persons to understand what common threads may exist among the target population.

Grounded theory aims to develop a theory based on information collected within a study (Tie et al., 2019; Yates & Leggett, 2016). Data is collected and analyzed, and themes are assigned. At the same time a researcher saturated in the environment and develops the themes identified to construct a new theory (LaRossa, 2005). My goal was not to produce a new theory but to understand events from the participants' perspectives.

Narrative research is a storytelling approach that focuses on details of life experiences (Andrews, 2021; Yates & Leggett, 2016). A researcher in narrative research meets with participants more than once to focus on obtaining the most in-depth information about their lives and experiences to accurately relay that information within the study (Yates & Leggett, 2016). As with the choice not to use a case study, the same reason applies to narrative research because the research questions required several participant experiences to understand what commonalities were found among several participants and entailed lengthy (i.e., 2-3 hours and or multiple sessions) interviews that made this approach not feasible for the study.

Population and Sample Selection

The population of interest was all female military veterans who have experienced MST in the United States. The target population of interest from which the sample was taken for this study was female veterans who experienced MST while on active duty and have sought mental health services for their post-active service trauma care in the United States. The sample consisted of female veterans with a history of using mental health care services after 2004 because that was the year that the Sexual Assault Task Force and Sexual Assault Prevention and Response programs were created and when universal screening for MST was adopted (Burgess et al., 2013; Calhoun et al., 2018; GonzalezPrats, 2017; Kimerling et al., 2007).

Limiting the years of service to 2004 and after assisted in identifying how the programs and services implemented after these changes were or were not beneficial within the identified veterans' lives.

Qualitative Sample Size

Mason (2010) suggested the existence of differing opinions about the sample size needed to conduct a qualitative study. Mason emphasized that utilizing many participants can be time-consuming because of the varying views collected. Saturation will occur when no new information is shared. Saturation will ensure repetitive data is not collected but that insight into the problem has been obtained (Cash et al., 2022; Mason, 2010).

Saturation occurs when no new information is collected.

Female veterans who have experienced military sexual trauma and sought services after 2004 were recruited from the Facebook, Instagram, and LinkedIn groups

Glass Soldier and the Facebook Military Sexual Trauma Movement Community Group

(see Appendix B) for this study. The original sample frame focused on recruiting at least 60 individuals, from which the sample for the survey will be at least 40 persons and a minimum of 15 to 20 individuals for the interview. To facilitate the minimum projected sample of 20 individuals, 10-12 persons were interviewed. The sample size allowed for attrition before, during, or after interviews and member-checking (Marcellus, 2004). Guest et al. (2006) reviewed numerous studies on sample size and qualitative methodology in their meta-study. The authors explained that while there are no specific parameters for sample size in qualitative methodology, some authors argued that 15 participants should be the smallest sample used for this methodology and six to eight interviews for a homogenous sample.

Recruiting and Sampling Strategy

Recruitment occurred through online veteran groups on social media websites such as Facebook, Instagram, and LinkedIn (see Appendix B). The recruitment letter contained the link to the anonymous online survey, where the Informed Consent document was the first screen on which participants either agreed or did not agree to continue to the survey. After the survey, participants accepted or denied if they wanted to be considered for the individual interviews. The online interview scheduling calendar link, Calendly (see Appendix G), was available when the participant chose yes for the individual interview. Nineteen participants who expressed interest in the personal interviews and who signed the Informed Consent were selected to continue with the study, from which 12 went forth with interviews. Two were asked to continue as alternates, one did not fully schedule their interview in Calendly, and four were noshows.

Initial contact was made with the gatekeeper of the online social media and online veteran groups to gain permission to post the link to the study's information and Informed Consent (see Appendix F). Site authorization was received and continued to be received in writing via each website's "private messaging" option to that site's administrator upon IRB approval to recruit and collect research data (see Appendix B). An explanation of my research, including the purpose and research questions, was shared at the request of the website administrator.

Sampling Strategy. Three strategy plans were carried out. Plan A for the sampling strategy was purposive. Plan B was snowball sampling. Plan C was convenience sampling.

Purposive sampling intentionally chooses study participants with experience and or backgrounds relevant to the study's purpose, problem statement, and research questions (Etikan et al., 2016; C. Parker et al., 2019). Utilizing purposive sampling results in obtaining the required information from participants until saturation is achieved (Guest et al., 2006). Female veterans who have served in any of the United States military branches, with a history of MST, and who have received mental health care for their trauma post-2004 were purposefully recruited.

Snowball sampling occurred when research participants were asked to recruit other participants who may have been a good fit for the study (Fink, 2003). Snowball sampling was important because it allowed me to access individuals who were not engaged in the primary recruiting method. The participants who had consented to the study shared the study's recruitment link with other individuals who they believed would also meet the participant criteria. Snowball sampling concluded once saturation was attained and the sample size was achieved (C. Parker et al., 2019).

Convenience sampling includes readily available individuals who will consent to the interview (Fink, 2003). Convenience samples are often called "accidental samples" because their location, proximity, availability, and accessibility benefit the researcher needing additional study participants (Etikan et al., 2016; Stratton, 2021). It is impossible to access the entire population related to the study, so the study is announced, and individuals can select whether they would like to attest to their participation (Stratton, 2021).

Sources of Data

Three sources of data were utilized. The first was the Quality-of-Life Scale (QOLS) questionnaire. Following the online QOLS, live interviews via the Zoom internet program (see Appendix G & H) were conducted. An additional data source was a reflection journal (see Appendix M). The participants were recruited through the online social media groups on LinkedIn, Instagram, and Facebook (see Appendix B).

Interview Protocol

The interview protocol consisted of 45 open- and closed-ended questions (see Appendix H), and each interview was scheduled for 60-90 minutes. Close-ended questions elicited yes or no answers but were followed up with open-ended questions for further clarity and specificity, as appropriate. Questions asked during the interviews were based on addressing the research questions for this study. Probing and follow-up questions during the interviews were asked for clarification and or to continue a participant statement (Van de Wiel, 2017). Maslow's hierarchy of needs (1943) and Deci and Ryan's (1985a) self-determination theories, the study's research questions, qualitative methodology, and descriptive design were considered when developing the interview protocol because it helped to determine what questions were asked, how they were asked, and ensured the interviews stayed on track (Turner & Hagstrom-Schmidt, 2022).

Research Data

Informed Consent and Recruitment Letter. The recruitment letter informed candidates about the study (see Appendix D). An additional recruitment flyer was used (see Appendix E). The informed consent document (see Appendix F) was administered through SurveyMonkey. All of these sources were used to obtain the research participants.

Questionnaires. The Quality-of-Life Scale (QOLS) questionnaire (see Appendix G) was used to facilitate questions to participants, and SurveyMonkey was used to administer the questionnaire to 20 participants. The QOLS questionnaire was developed by Flanagan (1978) and then later reconstructed by Burckhardt and Anderson (2003), and it is in the public domain, so permission was not required to use it in research or clinical practice. The questionnaire consists of 16 Likert-style questions that can be answered from 1-7 (1 is terrible, 2 is unhappy, 3 is mostly dissatisfied, 4 is mixed, 5 is mostly satisfied, 6 is pleased, and 7 is delighted). The final question on Survey Monkey© asked the participants if they wanted to participate in the individual interviews.

The QOLS measures several areas: material and physical well-being, relationships with others, social and community activities, personal development and fulfillment, recreation, and independence (Burckhardt &

Anderson, 2003). It is most often used in patients with chronic illnesses, but it has also been utilized for individuals with PTSD. In relation to PTSD, Balayan et al. (2014) suggested that QoL is increased when patients utilize some form of psychotherapy or pharmacotherapy. My aim was to understand whether QoL and well-being were affected by mental health care or other services. The data obtained from the survey assisted in understanding whether the participants thought there was a change in their QoL and or well-being since receiving services for the MST.

Individual Interviews. Individual interviews were conducted in a live session through the Zoom online platform. Each participant was sent a separate link and password to enter the interview session. The sample target was approximately 20 participants; 12 were interviewed. The interviews consisted primarily of open-ended questions with follow-up questions presented as needed and appropriate. The interview questions (see Appendix H) were based on RQ1 and RQ2 of the study, each question provided insight and guidance into the research questions.

Reflection Journals. The reflection journal (see Appendix M) was sent to the interviewed participants with a copy of their transcript for member-checking. The main purpose of the journal was to add anything they may have forgotten or wanted to add.

Thus, transparency was created within the process (Ortlipp, 2008).

Trustworthiness

Trustworthiness is attained in qualitative research by ensuring the quality of the study and confidence in the data presented (Connelly, 2016). It is established through protocol reviews (i.e., institutional reviews at several levels ending with a Dean's Read). An expert panel (see Appendix I) of terminally degreed individuals with some history or knowledge of military health care procedures, MST, non-military sexual trauma, or relevant experience reviewed the interview and questionnaire before they were utilized within the study (Elo et al., 2014). The expert panel review was used to ensure an evidence-based review (Coulter et al., 2016). Utilizing their professional expertise, each panelist provided feedback and suggested corrections to ensure that the study's purpose, research questions, and problem statement aligned with the interviews and questionnaires provided to the study candidates and participants. The panel reviews were completed, and interview questions were updated per the reviewers' suggestions.

Credibility

Connelly (2016) explained that credibility is the most important component of trustworthiness, as it establishes confidence in the truth of the presented study. Credibility is established by effective observation of the study participants, engagement over some time with the participants, debriefing, triangulation, journaling, and member-checking (Amankwaa, 2016). Credibility in the study was captured in the findings as to the "truth" of the participant statement relevant to the questionnaires and interviews that were conducted. It was important to ensure that the study accurately represented participants' experiences as they reported them. Once the transcripts from the interviews were transcribed, they were sent back to the participant for member-checking to ensure accuracy. Ensuring that saturation is reached can help with establishing credibility within the study.

Dependability

Dependability within a qualitative study refers to how stable the information remains as time passes (Connelly, 2016). The consistency of dependability indicates an ability to use the same or similar surveys, questionnaires, and research questions with the expected outcome to be trustworthy and credible (Amankwaa, 2016). Dependability in this study was achieved by ensuring that the method of thematic analysis was doublechecked with two methods for manual coding: (a) Saldaña (2009), and (b) patternmatching (Yin, 2009). Threats to dependability were minimized by ensuring that I maintain the process logs from the study for 3 years, ensuring room for an inquiry audit, and keeping an audit trail.

Transferability

Lemon and Hayes (2020) explained that transferability refers to how the data obtained from one study can also be applicable in other settings. A thick description provides detailed information about a phenomenon within a study and the conclusions made so that other deductions can be drawn within similar settings and contexts; a thick description is important in transferability (Amankwaa, 2016). Amankwaa also concluded that thick descriptions include observations made by the researcher and interactions with the research participants.

Transferability was achieved in this study by accurately describing the research data sources, their collection, protection, and analyses in detail for future replication (Elo et al., 2014). Information such as military branch, gender assigned at birth, MST reporting history, and services and support received were clearly stated. To minimize threats to transferability, participant details included their reactions, attitudes, bonds formed, any conflict presented, and information about the location, climate, atmosphere, and setting (Amankwaa, 2016).

Confirmability

Confirmability ensures that the research findings adequately represent the study participants rather than the researcher's bias (Lemon & Hayes, 2020). Detailed notes for all interactions were accomplished with field notes (i.e., a pad of paper and a pencil), and maintained in a locked safe in the researcher's personal residence to address threats to confirmability (Lemon & Hayes, 2020). Participants were sent a copy of their transcribed interview for member-checking (Connelly, 2016). Member-checking allows participants to ensure that their interview accurately reflects their intentions (Connelly, 2016).

Data Collection and Management

The data collection procedures are distinct for each of the three sources and ensure a robust triangulation for replication. The three sources included the survey (Quality of Life Scale; Appendix G), individual interviews (see Appendix H), and a reflection journal (see Appendix M). The Quality-of-Life scale (QOLS) was distributed via Survey Monkey©. The Informed Consent document was used for the survey and the confidential interviews and reflection journal (see Appendix H & M).

Data Collection for Informed Consent and Recruitment Letter

The Recruitment Letter was posted on Facebook, Instagram, and LinkedIn veteran groups and pages. The link in the Recruitment Letter (see Appendix D) took the participants to the anonymous Survey Monkey© survey, where the Informed Consent (see Appendix F) was the initial page. Participants had to agree or disagree to participate in the survey. If the participants agreed, they moved forward to complete the QOLS. If the participant disagreed, the survey ended there with no further information collected or requested.

At the end of the survey, the following statement appeared: To schedule your interview of 60 to 90 minutes about the services and support you are receiving or have received as a veteran, please click yes and then click next to continue to the next page where you will schedule your interview date and time. The link for Calendly was on the next page before the participant could end. The final step to submit was to click on the Calendly link (see Appendix G).

Data Collection for Survey and Interviews

The instrument in qualitative research is the principal investigator (PI), the researcher (Benjamin et al., 2022). Survey Monkey© distributed the Quality-of-Life Survey to the participants (see Appendix G). The results were anonymously delivered to me without the participant's IP address because the SurveyMonkey option not to collect was chosen. Interviews were conducted via the live Zoom internet platform, and sessions were password-protected. Participants scheduled their availability to interview from the link provided at the end of the Survey Monkey© survey or by emailing the principal investigator so that the link for Calendly could be sent to them (see Appendix G) to coincide with my interview availability via the online Calendly calendar.

The interviews conducted via Zoom provided a transcript for the principal investigator (PI), and an alternate program, Otter AI Meeting Assistant, was also used with Zoom. Both programs were used to confirm the interview audio. Paper and pen were used for notetaking during the audio-recorded interviews. Once transcribed, the PI further refined the audio recording transcript by listening to the playback and comparing it to the transcript (Lobe et al., 2020) before it was sent to the participant to member-check for accuracy (Ortlipp, 2008). The audio recordings and written notes have been stored in a password-protected safe (Roloway Brand) in the researcher's residence.

Data Collection for Reflection Journal

The reflection journal (see Appendix M) was distributed, and the interview transcript was sent to participants for member checking. The reflection journals were sent via email or to an address provided by participants through the United States Postal Service (USPS) with signature delivery. The participants could choose how they wanted to receive their transcripts delivered and how they wanted to return their reflection journals. If the participant opted to receive via USPS, an envelope (stamped and addressed to the researcher's PO Box address) was provided for return to me.

Research Data Protocol Procedures

Fifteen to 20 participants were recruited to complete the individual interviews. A link to the Informed Consent for the online, confidential survey and the live interview via Zoom was provided, and they were also read as a first item in the live interview before beginning. Due to the sensitive nature of this research, information packets were prepared with the names, addresses, and phone numbers for mental health supportive services in their area and online if additional support was needed for any signs of distress (see Appendix L). It was also made clear that participation in this study was voluntary, and participants could terminate their participation at any time during this research. The participants were monitored for distress at every step of the process to evaluate their mental health status regularly. These distress protocols involved questions about emotional distress, suicidality, homicidal ideation, and the need for immediate professional attention (Draucker et al., 2009). When researching sensitive topics, Draucker et al. (2009) indicated that distress protocols are necessary if the research has the potential to exacerbate emotional distress, such as anxiety, depression, embarrassment, and acute stress reactions. If there were any immediate needs, the participant would be directly linked to services (i.e., the interview may terminate, and local and or national hotline call numbers supplied). None of these immediate concerns were presented during this research process.

Interviews were conducted via Zoom, a private, password-protected platform where only me and the participant could access the room. Participants had already been informed that the interviews would be voice-recorded from the Informed Consent they reviewed. Still, the information was repeated, and the Informed Consent Participant Rights were read aloud to the participant before the interview began. Participants were also informed that once the transcript had been completed, they would be provided a copy to review for accuracy (i.e., member checking). Confidentiality was accomplished by storing the participant's identifying information separately from their responses to the interviews and questionnaire; code names were also assigned to increase confidentiality.

Management for Research Data Sources and Management

- Survey Monkey©: When the participants completed the questionnaire via Survey Monkey©, no IP addresses or phone numbers were collected to keep information secure and confidential. Information collected via the questionnaires has been kept on a password-protected USB drive and stored in a locked safe in the principal investigator's private residence. The information will be kept for a minimum of 3 years, and then it will be destroyed.

- Interview: The interviews were conducted via the online platform Zoom and were password-protected at the time of the interviews. The interview audio recordings have been kept on a password-protected USB drive and stored in a locked safe without personal identifiers. Code IDs were assigned to each participant to support confidentiality. The information will be kept for a minimum of 3 years, and then it will be destroyed.

- Reflection Journal: Reflection journals (see Appendix M) sent via email did not include identifying information (i.e., names, email addresses, etc.) on the journals. Reflection journals returned via physical mail had the principal investigators return information without indicating the participant's information. Information received via email has been stored on a password-protected USB and in a locked safe. Information received via physical mail has been stored in a locked cabinet.
  All information will be kept for at least 3 years and then destroyed.

Data Analysis Procedures

The purpose of the qualitative descriptive study was to understand how female military survivors of active-duty military sexual trauma who reside within the United States would describe the effects of their post-military provided mental health care services on their quality of life and well-being. To address the purpose of this study, the research questions (How do female veteran survivors of military sexual trauma describe their experiences with mental health services after discharge? and How do female veteran survivors of military sexual trauma describe the effects of post-military mental health services on their quality of life and well-being?) were applied. Using a questionnaire (see Appendix G), live interviews via Zoom online audio and visual platform (see Appendix G), and a reflection journal (see Appendix M), the research questions and responses were analyzed with the following procedures:

Manual Coding

Azungah (2018) described inductive reasoning as receiving information from participants to develop themes that can be pared down to the most important and salient theme or themes. In inductive reasoning, the researcher collects data to look for patterns among them and then tries to create a new theory based on the collected information (Kumar, 2024). Therefore, inductive reasoning was used to accomplish the coding process for the study. After research data was collected from the survey, the interviews, and reflection journals, coding and thematic analysis were used to analyze the collected data using the Saldaña (2009 & 2015) method and Yin pattern-matching (2009; Figure 2).

Saldaña (2009) and Yin (2009) explained that thematic analysis "analyzes and reports" themes within data (p. 79). The principal investigator read each source line by line to identify similarities between wording related to the research questions (Azungah, 2018). Using thematic analysis to identify similar themes allowed for the structural organization of the themes (Brooks et al., 2015). The phases of thematic analysis included transcribing the data, assigning initial codes, organizing the codes into possible themes, reviewing the themes identified, defining the themes, and reporting the data. As the principal investigator, I read and re-read the data, themes, and codes that continued to be pulled from the information until the process was exhausted (Saldaña, 2009, 2015).

Table 2

Sample Codebook

Code	Coding Cycle	Definition of Code
Services	1	MST services received
Level of difficulty	2	Difficulty locating/utilizing MH services
Type	3	Physical, verbal, emotional

The themes were categorized into those applicable to the study. Themes that were not applicable were discarded. Conclusions were drawn from the applicable themes that were represented and applied to the research questions.

RQ1: How do Thus, female veteran survivors of military sexual trauma describe their experiences with mental health care services after discharge?

RQ2: How do female veteran survivors of military sexual trauma describe the effects of post-military mental health care services on their quality of life and well-being?

To protect the participants' identities, they were assigned code names throughout the process (P1-P12). The steps for data analysis included the following three steps:

1. Transcripts were reviewed for pattern-matching using synonyms for some of the same words expressed directly relevant to MST (i.e., touching, misogynistic statements, and penetration).
2. Codes were categorized from the synonymic pattern-matching into distinct areas, such as verbal, emotional, and physical abuse.
3. Emerging themes, such as power, control, and fear, emerged from the transcripts. Related codes were combined into color-coded themes (Yin, 2009).

Pattern Coding and Pattern Matching. As noted, the first data analysis cycle utilized pattern coding and Yin's pattern matching (2009) techniques. Synonyms were pulled from the data collected, coded, and matched with similar counterparts. The information was color-coded to support identifying themed sets (see Figure 2).

Manual Descriptive Coding. As noted above, the next data analysis cycle utilized Saldaña's manual descriptive coding (2009, 2015). Saldaña described manual coding, which will involve transcribing the interviews and journals separately to find the emerging themes. It uses direct language from the interview transcripts and journals to preserve the participants' meanings of their beliefs, feelings, and thoughts. As Saldaña suggested, the principal investigator (PI) reviewed the data collected to group information into smaller themes.

Descriptive or topic coding summarizes the basic topic of the information received in a word or short phrase (Saldaña, 2009). Ensuring that the words or phrases directly reflected the information obtained in the interviews and reflection journals was important. Thus, themes accurately represented coding from participant interviews (see Appendix J).

Ethical Considerations

Ethical considerations are important when conducting research with human subjects. Ensuring that they are protected should be the top priority. The Belmont Report (1978) has contributed to developing ethical considerations and ethical standards for research, which must be followed when human subjects are present in a study (Kowalski et al., 2017; United States National Commission for the Protection of Human Subjects of Biomedical & Behavioral Research, 1978). This report lays the foundation for ethically sound research by mandating respect for persons, justice, and beneficence. Gabriele (2003) explained that respect for persons encompasses the right that every individual must make their own decisions without coercion or invalidation and the importance of protection for individuals who cannot decide for themselves. In this research study, respect for persons was obtained by ensuring confidentiality was maintained, and each participant was aware of their right to decline further participation at any time.

Participants were reminded, and it was clearly stated in the informed consent. Through validation and empathy, participants were not coerced or invalidated in reporting their experiences with services and support concerning MST.

Gabriele (2003) explained that justice should ensure that the risks and benefits are evenly distributed throughout the population. Justice was attained by ensuring that every participant knew the risks and benefits accompanying their acceptance into the study. Beneficence reminds the researcher to "do no harm" and always to have the best interest of the study participants at the forefront of one's mind (Gabriele, 2003). Maximizing benefits and minimizing harm is the goal (Adashi et al., 2018). The focus is to ensure that study participants, particularly vulnerable populations, are not harmed (Adashi et al.,
2018). Beneficence was obtained by ensuring that no harm was done to the participants. Establishing the distress protocol before beginning any research with the participants was beneficial to ensuring that there was a plan in place in case anyone began to experience distress, and the resources were revisited often throughout the process.

Research implications and future use of information must be transparent, and research participants must be allowed to make an informed decision about participation based on the research parameters (Friesen et al., 2017). The authors further explained that the Belmont Report (1978) emphasizes that research should enhance participants' wellbeing and contribute to "generalizable knowledge." The study planned to utilize online veteran groups through Facebook, Instagram, and or LinkedIn and private and public veteran groups to recruit research participants. Site authorization was obtained through meeting with the gatekeeper to explain the purpose of the study and the desire to recruit from the group.

Keogh and Daly (2009) explained that the gatekeeper advocates for the research participants, or vulnerable population, that the researcher is studying and ensures that ethical integrity is upheld. Obtaining IRB approval was the first task to protect the research participants, and the data received. Obtaining informed consent from each participant was imperative because it allowed them to make an informed decision about whether they wanted to participate in this study and their rights to participation and to discontinue participation (Kay et al., 2015). The informed consent fully explained the research, its goals, the risks, the benefits associated with their participation, and any capacity in which the results could be utilized in the future (Schulte & Sweeney, 1995). Participants were reminded verbally and in writing on their informed consent that their participation in the research was voluntary and that they were able to end their participation at any time without any penalties.

This study posed both risks and benefits. The most apparent was the risk of increased distress due to the nature of the research. As explained by Draucker et al. (2009), distress protocols are important because they assess emotional distress, suicidality, homicidal ideation, and the need for immediate professional attention. A list of mental health and crisis resources relevant to the geographic location was assembled and provided to each study participant (see Appendix L). Participants were also well informed throughout the study that they could end the interview whenever they chose. I remained aware and vigilant in reacting to any triggering questions or comments due to the sensitivity of the information provided by participants.

The study's principal investigator is a licensed therapist and was able to ascertain when an interview needed to end. My profession also allowed me to pause due to distress and possibly begin at another time. The benefits of the study included furthering the knowledge of others regarding services and support that may be effective in increasing well-being and QoL after military sexual trauma.

The data obtained through the research has been stored on a flash drive and locked in a safe and locked cabinet. Only I have access to the safe, cabinet, and flash drive information. The book committee, IRB representatives, and or college representatives were granted access to these records to verify the information collected and analyzed.

The information will be kept for 3 years post-completion if it needs to be retrieved, and then it will be destroyed. Any identifying information that could be linked to the study participants has been coded, with the codes stored in a separate location from the data (on a separate flash drive in a separate locked location). After 3 years, any paperwork will be shredded and recycled, ensuring that no information is thrown away in a regular garbage bin. Electronic records will be erased using the appropriate computer software and then physically destroyed (University of Virginia, 2021).

Assumptions and Delimitations

This section aims to identify and specify this study's assumptions and delimitations. Assumptions are ideas the researcher accepts as true without established proof (Ellis & Levy, 2009; Simon & Goes, 2013). The assumptions listed here are ideas assumed to be true about the study. Delimitations are factors and variables the researcher has control over and makes specific choices about (Ellis & Levy, 2009; Simon & Goes, 2013). This section lists the assumptions and delimitations and a brief explanation of each.

Assumptions

The following assumptions were applied:

- It was assumed that research participants truthfully represented themselves as female military veterans who are MST survivors. Participants were not rewarded for their participation and did not have any gain to participate in this study.

- It was assumed that the research participants answered interview and questionnaire questions honestly based on their experiences and beliefs. An expert panel approved the questions. To help facilitate my assumption, the study participants' names and identities will be kept confidential for no less than 3 years.

Delimitations

The following delimitations were present in this study:

- To increase the number of participants, I recruited participants from local online veteran groups through Facebook, Instagram, and LinkedIn. Specific inclusion and exclusion criteria were used to ensure all participants understood the requirements and could add to the data collection measures.

- Participants were limited to female veterans who served in the military since 2004. This delimitation excluded male veterans as well as any veteran who is a survivor of MST and served before 2004. Veterans since 2004 were used to represent veterans who were serving once the Sexual Assault Prevention and Response (SAPR) program was established.

- Data collection methods were delimited to questionnaires, interviews, and reflection journals, purposely excluding other methods.

- Participants were limited to those who resided within the United States. Although MST occurs in other countries, this study only included those residing in the United States at the time of their participation.

The participants were random, which limits the study's transferability. Because of its limitations, the study is not generalizable. It would be difficult to replicate the study because of confidentiality, anonymity, and the participants' locations.

Summary

The purpose of this qualitative descriptive study was to explore the experiences of female veteran survivors of military sexual trauma with mental health services and to investigate veterans' perceived quality of life outcomes from these mental health services who reside within the United States. Chapter 3 provided a detailed review of the methodology and design, population, sample and selection, instruments and sources of data, data collection, and data analysis. The qualitative methodology and descriptive design were chosen to allow for an understanding of the attitudes and experiences of the participants (McCusker & Gunaydin, 2015).

A Quality-of-Life survey (QOLS), individual interviews, and a reflection journal were utilized for data collection. Female veterans who have served in any military branches since 2004 within the United States comprised the sample. A purposive sample of 40-60 participants were contacted through online veteran's groups or pages from Facebook, LinkedIn, and or Instagram. This sample yielded a total of 20 participants. Manual coding was done using Saldaña's manual coding (2009) and Yin patternmatching (2009) to determine themes consistent with the research questions. Chapter 4 includes data analysis and results, data preparation and procedures for analyses, the results, limitations, and the final chapter summary.

Chapter 4: Data Analysis and Results

Introduction

The purpose of this qualitative descriptive study was to understand how female military survivors of active-duty military sexual trauma who reside within the United States would describe the effects of their post-military provided mental health care services on their quality of life and well-being. Holland et al. (2016) and Kintzle et al. (2015) strongly suggested that more research was necessary to understand the mental health services needed for female military veterans who experienced MST while on active duty. Matt et al. (2020) suggested that further research focus on the facets of care that benefit veteran survivors of MST. At the time I began my study, I did not know how female military survivors of active-duty military sexual trauma would describe the effects of their post-military provided mental health care services on their quality of life and well-being. The phenomenon I studied was how mental health services received after MST contributed to the female veterans' perceptions of QoL and well-being after discharge from the military.

The following research questions guided this study:

RQ1: How do female veteran survivors of military sexual trauma describe their experiences with mental health care services after discharge?

RQ2: How do female veteran survivors of military sexual trauma describe the effects of post-military mental health care services on their quality of life and well-being?

Chapter 4 will explain the qualitative descriptive findings of the study. It will explain the process I used to collect and prepare the research data in a step-by-step analysis. It will also inform you of the changes during the process that differed from the information outlined in Chapter 3. The results of the qualitative descriptive study will be presented. The data analysis procedures and steps will be explained, and the themes that emerged from the data will be presented and explained. The limitations of the study will be discussed, and the chapter will end with a chapter summary.

Important Changes and Updates to Information in Chapters 1-3

Changes were made during the data collection and analysis process that deviated from the original research plan presented in Chapters 1-3. Female veterans who served in the United States military in 2004 or beyond with an experience of military sexual trauma and who sought mental health care services for that trauma after their military discharge as veterans were the focus of this study. The goal was to recruit participants by posting the recruitment letter in the Facebook, Instagram, and LinkedIn groups that initially granted permission to recruit. Those groups were: The Glass Solider and the Military Sexual Trauma Movement Community group. After 3 weeks, only a few female veterans signed up for the study. I then created a recruitment flyer with important information about the study, contact information, a link, and a QR code to the Informed Consent and survey to better catch the eye of the candidates (e.g., recruitment letter) and participants (e.g., informed consent) and to more concisely explain the research purpose and how to participate. After the Grand Canyon University IRB approved the new flyer, it was again posted on the Facebook, Instagram, and LinkedIn groups and pages once the gatekeepers reapproved it. The slight change in the recruitment plan helped to increase the number of participants for this study.

The target sample, originally presented in Chapter 3, aimed to recruit at least 60 individuals, where at least 40 would be recruited to complete the Quality-of-Life survey (QOLS), and the other 15-20 individuals would then be recruited for the semi-structured, open-ended interviews. The study's minimum projected sample was 20 individuals, with at least 10-12 participating in the interviews. The target sample size was not achieved using plan A, purposive sampling, plan B snowball sampling, and plan C convenience sampling. In total, the minimum projected sample size of 20 was achieved, but the study did not meet the anticipated recruitment of at least 60 individuals. In total, 20 female veterans were recruited; 12 were interviewed, and all 20 completed the online QoL Survey (QOLS). Although the projected sample size was not achieved, the research questions were thoroughly answered, and data saturation was achieved before interviewing all 12 participants. The data showed that the important issues and insights were exhausted (Hennink & Kaiser, 2022).

The original data analysis plan was to manually code using Saldaña's manual coding and Yin's pattern matching without using coding software. Although the coding techniques did not change, MAXQDA was used to code manually; no automated assistance was utilized from the MAXQDA program. I also utilized manual coding with pen and paper. Due to the complexities of the data analysis, this change was necessary to assist in keeping the collected research data better organized. The MAXQDA software allowed for a more detailed visual representation of the collected data and still allowed me to color-code the information in the software and on paper when needed.

Preparation of Raw Data for Analysis and Descriptive Data

Preparation of Raw Data for Analysis

The preparation of raw data for analysis in this study was completed in several steps, beginning with posting the Informed Consent (see Appendix F) in the Facebook, Instagram, and LinkedIn groups and pages preapproved by the gatekeepers. The informed consent was posted online and collected as each participant completed it. After agreeing to participate in the study, the participants were led to the online Quality of Life Survey (QOLS), where they answered 16 Likert-style questions (see Appendix G) measuring quality of life in material and physical well-being, relationships with others, social and community activities, personal development and fulfillment, recreation, and independence (Burckhardt & Anderson, 2003). The participants who indicated a "yes" to participate in the interviews at the end of the QOLS were assigned an alphanumeric code
(P1-P12) and were only referred to by this code throughout the remainder of the study.

The participants who opted to complete the online individual semi-structured interviews scheduled a Zoom meeting using the Calendly app with the link provided at the end of the QOLS. On their scheduled date and time, the participant entered the Zoom meeting and was asked to update their name to their assigned participant's alphanumeric code. Before recording, introductions were completed, and the participant verbally consented to the interview audio recording. After the consent was given, interviews immediately began. At the beginning of the interviews, I read the participants' rights directly from the Informed Consent, in which the participant reconfirmed their understanding and immediately had the option to ask any questions. Once questions and or concerns were answered, the semi-structured interview with each participant began (see Appendix K). The interviews were audio recorded via the Zoom platform, and the written transcription was provided both by the Zoom platform and through the use of the Otter AI Meeting Assistant transcription program. The participants' information was also coded in the applications utilizing their alphanumeric code. I used paper and pen during the interviews to capture nonverbal cues such as laughter, smiling, and signs of distress, as these cues are difficult to revisit through the transcription or without a video recording (McMullin, 2023).

Following completion of the interviews, the audio recordings were uploaded to my personal, password-protected USB drive and labeled with each participant's alphanumeric code. Also included in the file name was the date and time of the interview, for example, P5_8.25.24_12pm, and saved in a file folder on the USB drive entitled "participants." Once uploaded to the password-protected USB drive, the audio recordings were deleted from the Zoom platform. I then began refining the audio recording transcripts by listening to the playback and comparing it to the transcript line-by-line (Lobe et al., 2020). Minimal changes were made to the transcripts, only to correct wrongly transcribed words. After verifying accurate transcription, the transcripts were sent to the participants for member-checking via their preferred return. Eleven participants opted for an email return, while one opted to have it mailed to their home via United States Postal Service delivery with tracking, signature delivery, and a selfaddressed, stamped return envelope.

The interview information collected produced three versions of each participant's transcript. The first version was the raw transcript without any corrections. They came directly from the Otter AI application. The second version was produced after I read and listened to the audio-recorded transcripts, line-by-line and made any necessary changes according to the audio recordings. This version of the transcript was the one sent to the participant for member-checking. The third version was the transcript sent back from the participants with updates or corrections. Only one transcript was returned with updates. Version two of the transcripts was used for manual coding for eleven participants, while version three was used for the participant who returned the transcript with minor updates with the reflection journal. The Zoom audio recordings from the interviews and the AQR transcripts (single-spaced) were uploaded to the DC Network under the Learner's

book Page.

Descriptive Data

The online veteran's groups and page gatekeepers were contacted for permission to recruit and conduct the study (see Appendix B). The private Facebook group, Military Sexual Trauma Movement Community, the Glass Soldier's LinkedIn, Instagram, and Facebook pages were contacted and provided with the Informed Consent document outlining the study's protocol and how confidentiality would be ensured. After the permissions were given and the Grand Canyon University IRB approved the study, the recruitment process began by posting the informed consent and, later, the study flyer to the social media groups and pages with the gatekeepers' approvals.

As the informed consent documents were completed with the Survey Monkey© survey and interviews were scheduled, participants were immediately given an alphanumeric identification code so their identities could not be traced back to their surveys and interviews. I was the only person with access to the identifiers. The redacted information was reported to the Grand Canyon University book committee and reviewers. My personal contact information was provided to the participants throughout this process, on the recruitment flyer, and after the surveys were completed in case of any questions or concerns. The primary data sources for this research were the Survey Monkey© survey responses, the individual interviews completed through the online Zoom platform, and any reflection journals returned (see Appendix M).

The two research questions that guided this study were the focus of the information collected through the online survey, the individual interviews, and the reflection journal. The questions are:

RQ1: How do female veteran survivors of military sexual trauma describe their experiences with mental health care services after discharge?

RQ2: How do female veteran survivors of military sexual trauma describe the effects of post-military mental health care services on their quality of life and well-being?

The primary data sources were utilized to provide information relevant to the research questions and to understand how female military survivors of active-duty military sexual trauma would describe the effects of their post-military provided mental health care on their quality of life and well-being. The reflection journals were optional for participants who wanted to add information to their interviews that they may have forgotten or wanted to elaborate more after reading their interview transcript (see Appendix M). Due to the sensitive nature of the research, the individual interviews were not video recorded; they were only audio recorded. Notes were taken with pen and paper to note any nonverbal cues, changes in expression, or clues that could not be picked up through only the audio recording.

Some non-verbal communication and cues observed included sighing, tearing up or crying, looking down or away from me, the participant wiping their eyes, or hesitancy to answer a question. For full disclosure, I am a licensed therapist, trained and wellexperienced in verbal cues as part of my basic therapy training. These nonverbal cues could indicate distress, needing additional time to gather themselves, reflection, or needing more time to think. It was important to remain mindful of these cues to determine whether changes needed to be made, such as allowing a pause in the interview, checking in about their current mental health, and even ending the interview early. Remaining vigilant for these cues was important in the process. It was a part of the distress protocol that was planned for and utilized with each participant because of the sensitive nature of this study (Draucker et al., 2009). This information was also important when transcribing and presenting the information.

The participants were in different parts of their journey with mental health care following their encounter with military sexual trauma. Some had been discharged from the military longer than others, so their care began several years ago. In contrast, others were recently discharged and were beginning to engage in their mental health care services. Although their time with treatment and the treatment they received may have been different, they were connected because of their shared experiences as survivors of MST. Some of the repeated words by the participants included positive, difficult, emotional, anxiety, helpful, support, wrong, stress, overwhelming, wait, and depression when talking about their engagement with mental health care services for MST after their military discharge. Other repeated words included community, journal, medication, CBT (cognitive behavioral therapy), EMDR (Eye Movement Desensitization and Reprocessing), and yoga when discussing the actual mental health care services and support they received. Noted and repeated is that confidentiality was important because of the sensitive nature of the research.

Accompanying the strategies to ensure confidentiality, two password-protected USBs were utilized to store participant recordings and personal information and the other with their coded information. When not used by me, the USBs and other notes from the individual interviews were locked in a file cabinet in my personal residence. It was explained to the participants that the collected information would be locked up and kept for at least 3 years in the researcher's personal residence.

Data Collection

Participants

The interview participants were female veterans from different military eras, branches, and regions of the United States (see Table 3). Their service averaged 11.58 years, with service spanning from 1988 through 2023. All veterans who participated in this study were discharged from the military in 2004 or later. Their discharge codes were all honorable, some retired, and some medically discharged. Three of the six military branches were represented, although the Army was mostly represented. Most of the female veteran participants in this study were domiciled in the Southern part of the United States of America. Both enlisted (ranks of E1-E7) and officer-ranking veterans participated in the study, although the majority were previously enlisted members of the armed forces.

Table 3

Participant Demographics, Female Veterans

Participants (*n*=12)	Location in the U.S	Military Branch	Years Served	Discharge Type	Rank at Discharge
Participant 1	Northeastern	Navy	2005-2019	Medical/Honorable	E6
Participant 2	Southcentral	Army	2009-2017	Medical/Honorable	E4
Participant 3	Northeastern	Army	2011-2016	Medical/Honorable	Captain/O3
Participant 4	Northwestern	Air Force	2014-2017	Medical/Honorable	E3
Participant 5	Southcentral	Army	2007-2011	Medical/Honorable	E4
Participant 6	Southeastern	Army	1988-2021	Retired/Honorable	E7
Participant 7	Southeastern	Army	2003-2011	Honorable	E6
Participant 8	Southeastern	Army	1996-2005	Medical/Honorable	E5
Participant 9	Northwestern	Navy	2013-2018	Honorable	E5
Participant 10	Southeastern	Army	1998-2019	Retired/Honorable	E7
Participant 11	Southeastern	Army	2001-2023	Retired/Honorable	Major/O4
Participant 12	Southeastern	Army	2001-2009	Honorable	E6

Once the proposed participants had some interest in possibly participating in the study, they clicked on the link or scanned the QR code located on the recruitment letter or study flyer, and then the data collection process began. The first step was reading the

Informed Consent (see Appendix F) at the beginning of the Survey Monkey© survey. The Informed Consent informed the potential participants of the eligibility criteria to be able to participate in the study. The Informed Consent addressed what the participants would be asked to do if they chose to participate, the risks and benefits, how the study would be conducted, privacy and data security, and participants' rights. If the participants agreed to the Informed Consent, they acknowledged by entering their name and the date, and then they were granted access to the Quality-of-Life survey (QOLS; Appendix G), administered through Survey Monkey©. If they disagreed, the survey ended immediately. A total of 20 participants agreed to participate in the online survey and submitted their Informed Consent (See Figure 3). Not all of them participated in the semi-structured interviews.

Figure 3

Agreement to Participate

Voluntary ConsentParticipant Rights· You have been given an opportunity to read and discuss the informed consent and ask questions about this study.· You have been given enough time to consider whether or not you want to participate.· You have read and understand the terms and conditions and agree to take part in this research study.· You understand your participation is voluntary and that you may stop participation at any time without penalty.

Answered: 20 Skipped: 0

ANSWER CHOICES		RESPONSES
If you have read the Informed Consent and agree to participate in this study, please type your First and Last name in the box	Responses	100.00% 20
Please enter today's date	Responses	100.00% 20

Quality of Life Survey (QOLS)

The Quality-of-Life Survey (QOLS) was utilized for this study (see Appendix G).

The QOLS was initially developed by Flanagan in 1978 and was later reconstructed by Burckhardt and Anderson (2003). The reconstructed questionnaire was used in this study and administered via SurveyMonkey©. There are 16 Likert-style questions measuring the quality of life in material and physical well-being, relationships with others, social and community activities, personal development and fulfillment, recreation, and independence (Burckhardt & Anderson, 2003). The participants were asked to answer questions about how these specific areas of their lives are now on a scale of 1-7 after receiving their mental health care for MST specifically. The results of the QOLS primarily consisted of mixed (score of 4), mostly satisfied (score of 5), and pleased (score of 6), with participants feeling differently in these areas of their lives as they pertained to quality of life (see Appendix G). Figure 4 shows a sample of the results for a question on the QOLS.

Figure 4

Quality of Life Survey (QOLS) Result Examples

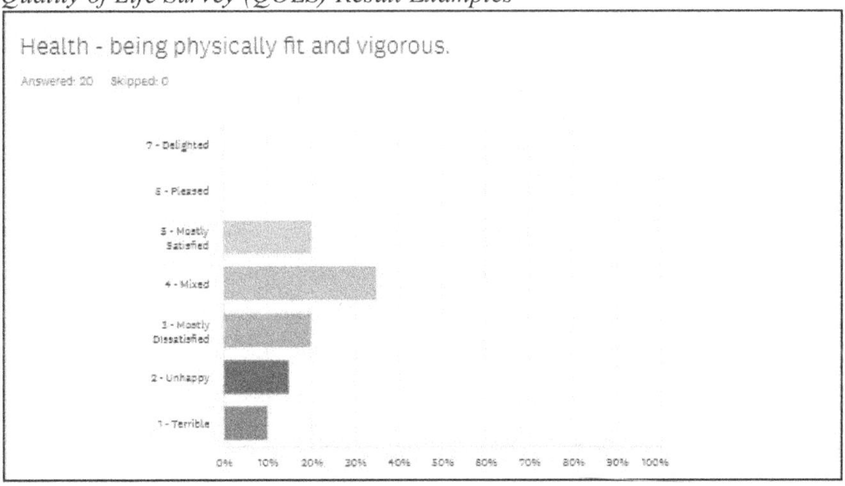

The goal was sixty individuals, 40 for the surveys and 15-20 for the interviews. The recruitment plan was to meet the study's minimum projected sample of 20 individuals and a minimum of 10-12 persons for interviews to account for attrition

(Marcellus, 2004). Twenty participants completed the Informed Consent and the SurveyMonkey© surveys. The questionnaire was between 2 minutes and 15 seconds and

1,252 minutes and 39 seconds (see Table 4).

Table 4

Survey Monkey© Questionnaire, Duration for Completion

Survey	Setting	Date	Duration	Participated in individual interview
Survey 1	Survey Monkey©	07/24/2024	2:55	Yes
Survey 2	Survey Monkey©	07/29/2024	20:52:24	No
Survey 3	Survey Monkey©	08/09/2024	6:04	Yes
Survey 4	Survey Monkey©	08/09/2024	1:35:39	No
Survey 5	Survey Monkey©	08/11/2024	2:15	Yes
Survey 6	Survey Monkey©	08/20/2024	5:43	Yes
Survey 7	Survey Monkey©	08/24/2024	9:09	Yes
Survey 8	Survey Monkey©	08/24/2024	3:27	Yes
Survey 9	Survey Monkey©	08/25/2024	3:31	Yes
Survey 10	Survey Monkey©	08/25/2024	3:15	No
Survey 11	Survey Monkey©	09/04/2024	7:34	No
Survey 12	Survey Monkey©	09/05/2024	5:35	No
Survey 13	Survey Monkey©	09/06/2024	35:41	Yes
Survey 14	Survey Monkey©	09/07/2024	16:26	No
Survey 15	Survey Monkey©	09/07/2024	4:25	Yes
Survey 16	Survey Monkey©	09/09/2024	7:13	Yes
Survey 17	Survey Monkey©	09/09/2024	8:51	Yes
Survey 18	Survey Monkey©	10/04/2024	2:49	Yes
Survey 19	Survey Monkey©	11/16/2024	4:35	No
Survey 20	Survey Monkey©	11/22/2024	2:37	No
MEAN	N/A	N/A	…	10

TOTAL	N/A	N/A	33	12

At the end of the survey, participants were allowed to schedule their interviews using the provided link to Calendly (see Appendix G), which routed participants to a separate site to schedule. When the participant clicked the Calendly link, several options for flexibility were provided on different days and times. The Calendly link required the participant to enter their personal information, including their first and last name and email address. A total of 19 participants out of the 20 who completed the survey opted to participate in the interviews.

Interviews

Once the 20 participants completed the online survey, they could opt to complete the individual interviews. The individual semi-structured interviews were to be completed through the Zoom online platform at a later date and time of the participants' choosing. Of the 20 participants who completed the surveys, 19 opted into the semistructured open-ended individual interviews (see Figure 5), but only 18 proceeded to the online Calendly app to schedule.

Figure 5

Agreement to Participate in Individual Interviews

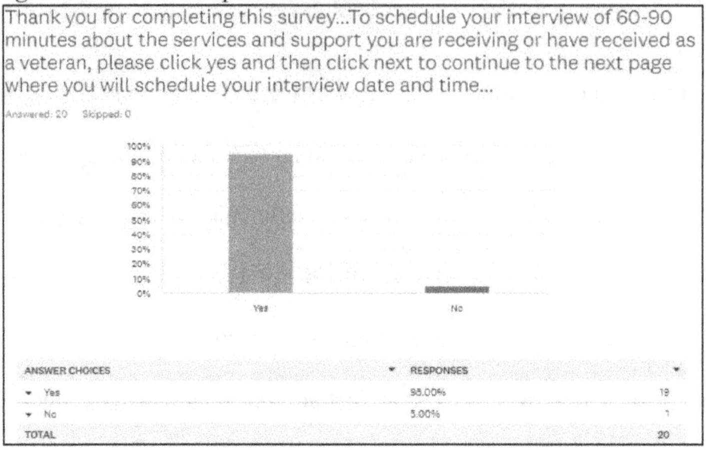

I did not conduct face-to-face individual interviews because the survey was open to all female veterans who resided within the United States, and it was not feasible to carry out. Communication was limited to email once the interviews were completed. Participants were given this researcher's email address and phone number for telephone calls or text messages. The purpose of this qualitative descriptive study was to understand how female military survivors of active-duty military sexual trauma who reside within the United States would describe the effects of their post-military provided mental health care services on their quality of life and well-being. This research did not store the personal demographic data obtained for a statistical profile of participants in the same place as their identifying information, because two USB port external drives were used. Participant codes were immediately assigned to each participant in the individual interviews.

As noted, there were 20 survey participants on Survey Monkey©; 12 completed the confidential semi-structured individual interviews. One interview was not scheduled, although they opted to participate, because they did not fully complete the Calendly request for an interview, so their contact information was not captured. Two participants served as alternates due to the later timing of their survey completions. Four participants were no-shows for the interview on their scheduled day and time, and one opted not to participate in the individual interview. The first participant who completed the interview was given a P1 code, which indicates participant number one. This letter and numbering continued until P12 was achieved, representing the 12 individual interview participants.

The individual interviews were conducted over the Zoom online platform under a password-protected link. There were 45 questions in the interview (see Appendix G), ranging from a few basic demographic questions to questions aimed at understanding more about the participants' enlistment in the military to specific questions about the mental health care services and support they received. The interviews ranged from 50 minutes-13 seconds to 1 hour 39 minutes-51 seconds. The average interview duration was 1 hour 8 minutes-39 seconds. The transcribed interview responses ranged from 3-14 pages, single-spaced in Times New Roman 12 font. Appendix K displays a sample of the interview transcript. The interview and transcript data are listed in Table 5.

Table 5

Interview Times and Length

Participant	Interview Date	Interview Duration	# Transcript Pages (Times New Roman, 12, single spaced)	Survey Completed	Reflection Journal Returned

Participant 1	08/07/24	77:26	11	Yes	No
Participant 2	08/12/24	64:28	6	Yes	No
Participant 3	08/15/24	58:37	5	Yes	No
Participant 4	08/25/24	74:25	13	Yes	No
Participant 5	08/25/24	56:18	5	Yes	No
Participant 6	08/29/24	50:13	3	Yes	No
Participant 7	09/08/24	109:51	14	Yes	Yes
Participant 8	09/09/24	52:34	5	Yes	No
Participant 9	09/14/24	54:48	6	Yes	No
Participant 10	09/14/24	74:21	7	Yes	No
Participant 11	09/15/24	87:32	9	Yes	No
Participant 12	10/23/24	62:36	6	Yes	No
MEAN	N/A	68:39	7.5	12	0.083
TOTAL	12	823:09	90	12	1

During the online interviews, notes were taken using pen and paper to capture visual cues. I observed specifically for visual cues such as changes in facial expressions, responses to specific questions or answers, specific movements, and any other visual changes displaying possible distress or feelings of discomfort. These visual cues were used to guide the interviews and served to continue to build rapport throughout the interview process (Mirick & Wladkowski, 2019).

Reflection Journal

After the 12 interviews were transcribed and checked for verbatim program transcription, the interview transcripts were sent to participants for member-checking along with the reflection journals (see Appendix M). The reflection journals served as an additional data source, though not a primary source. The reflection journals allowed the interviewed participants to expand upon or add to the information previously captured in the individual interviews (Ortlipp, 2008). At the top of the reflection journal, the instructions read:

> Please read and review the enclosed interview transcript from our Zoom interview on (the interview date was entered). Use this reflection journal to include any additional information you think was not included in the interview. If there is something that came to mind following our interview that you would like to share, please include it here. If there is nothing else you would like to add, please indicate "no new information" in the area below and return it to me.
>
> If you have any questions or concerns, please do not hesitate to contact me (my contact information was listed).

Out of the 12 reflection journals sent with the transcripts for member-checking, only one was returned. This reflection journal added information not included in the original interview transcript. The reflection journal brought to light the difficulties with receiving mental health care services if the veteran decided not to report the assault. It went on to discuss how that would be another barrier to improving one's QoL and or well-being, because veteran care services would be denied without at least a verbal report.

Data Analysis Procedures

The goal of this research was to understand how female military survivors of active-duty military sexual trauma described the effects of their post-military provided mental health care on their quality of life (QoL) and well-being. The female veterans who were invited to participate in this study could have served in any branch of the United States Armed Forces, experienced MST while enlisted, and sought mental health care services after discharge as veterans. To meet the study's requirements, the female veterans had to be enlisted (e.g., active duty) during or after 2004 due to the implementation of the Sexual Assault Prevention and Response Office (SAPRO). As noted earlier in this study, the SAPRO is responsible for implementing guidelines for all military branches in their prevention and response training for MST (Gonzalez-Prats, 2017; Lofgreen, 2020).

Manual descriptive coding was utilized for the data analysis of this study. I used Saldaña's (2009) manual coding and Yin's (2009) pattern matching to identify codes, themes, and narratives. The data analysis procedures were applied to the questionnaires, individual interviews, and the reflection journal. The data was analyzed to answer the two research questions and the problem statement that guided this study. MAXQDA software and pen and paper were both utilized to code manually. MAXQDA supported my analysis by keeping the coded information better organized; however, I also utilized manual coding. Figure 6 shows the process utilized to code the primary data sources.

Figure 6

Saldaña's Thematic Analysis Approach for Recognizing Themes in Qualitative Data

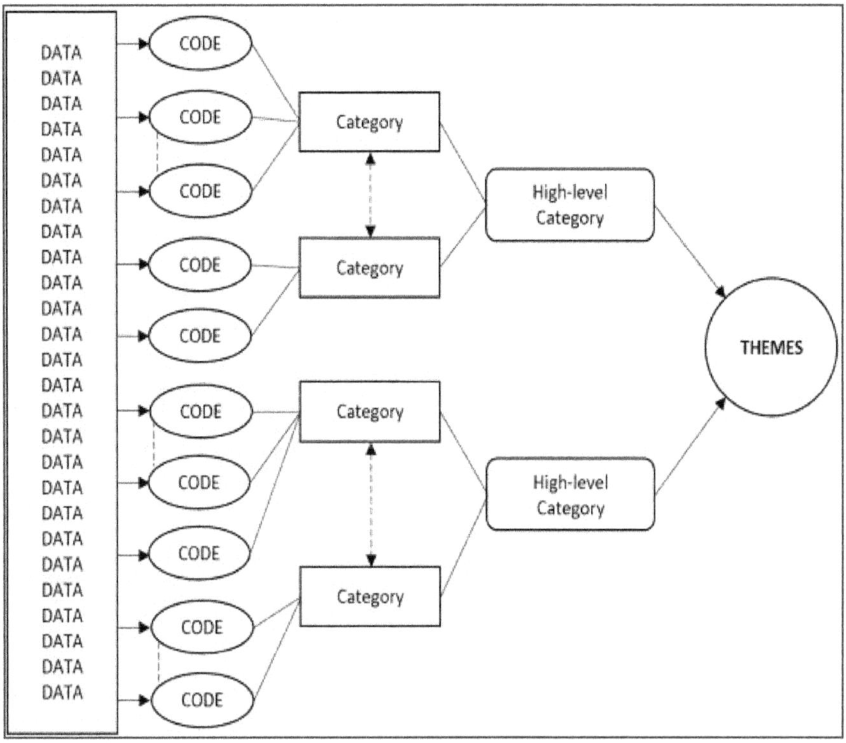

Note. From Amanfi (2019). Used with permission, see Appendix N.

Reflexivity Protocol

Reflexivity protocols were used to track and manage the possible researcher bias that may have influenced the research process. The reflexivity process served as a way to promote introspection along the way (Patnaik, 2013). It is essential to understand that a researcher plays a large part in the research outcome if not aware of their experiences, attitudes, and emotions (Patnaik, 2013). This researcher thought it was important to review personal biases and experiences that could influence the research to neutralize the effects of subjectivity (Olmos-Vega et al., 2023). It was also important to be aware of each interaction with every participant or potential participant to ensure personal biases and past experiences did not influence the participants.

Bracketing was utilized to come to the research with a "blank slate" (Olmos-Vega et al., 2023, p. 242). Bracketing helps to decrease the assumptions that may accompany a researcher when engaging with the research participants (Habibullah et al., 2023). The author further explained that it is crucial for a researcher to first identify the bias and possible preconceptions before engaging with the participant to be more fully present in the raw data collection. Habibullah et al. (2023) also explained that extensive research on a delicate topic might drain a researcher and make it difficult to continue without bias.

Bracketing proved to be an important process for this research study.

The individual experiences and biases identified included the researcher's professional experience as a mental health therapist and Army veteran. This researcher currently works as a mental health therapist, collaborating with veterans, some of whom have experienced trauma and require trauma therapy. I mitigated this area by not recruiting participants from the personal work site. Also, I did not recruit veterans who were personally known to me from previous or current mental health therapy or any fellow veterans I may have previously served with while on active Army duty.

This researcher served in the United States Army from 2001 to 2003. To mitigate this bias, this researcher ensured that no one was personally recruited for the study who this researcher knew to have experienced MST.

The research participants were recruited from online social media platforms: Facebook, Instagram, and LinkedIn. Permission was first granted by the gatekeepers of each group, where the recruitment letter and flyer (see Appendix E and F) were posted. This helped eliminate the bias of choosing participants based on prior knowledge about their experiences.

Utilizing an expert panel to review research questions assisted in decreasing the probability of the researcher's bias and influence and ensured objectivity. Open-ended questions were at the forefront of the interviews. The open-ended questions allowed the interview to remain evidence-based (Coulter et al., 2016). They supported the participants in leading the interviews, sharing, and discussing what was comfortable for them. Member-checking, or the participants' review of their transcripts, was completed to ensure that the information captured in the interviews accurately reflected their intentions (Connelly, 2016). This was important in building and maintaining rapport throughout the process.

Before engaging with each interview participant, this researcher reviewed notes made about personal bias and experiences. I was reminded that the interviews were not for professional psychotherapy services to aid in supporting the interaction through the lens of a researcher rather than a mental health therapist. During each interview, I thought it was important to listen and support through empathy due to the sensitive nature of the research topic, but to also remember that there is a fine line to maintaining the role of a researcher and not a therapist in the process (Burkard & Knox, 2014). After each interview, this researcher wrote notes about things that went well and areas that could be improved for the following participant interview. The expert panel reviewers remained available to this researcher throughout this process for any additional support in this area, if needed, although they were not utilized.

Data Analysis Steps

Inductive reasoning was used to look for patterns and identify themes in the data collected (Azungah, 2018). Through inductive reasoning, the collected data through the individual interviews and the reflection journal identified the themes through repetitive data review and collection. Through inductive reasoning, the raw data uncovers codes utilized to determine the themes within the research data. The iterative process of inductive analysis involved multiple reviews of each transcript and refining codes several times to ensure codes were not missed so that themes reflective of the codes would be produced (Vears & Gillam, 2022). Table 6 shows some codes developed through the initial data collection process.

Table 6

Inductive Analysis

Code	Description of Code	Examples from Transcript
Problems with trust	How the effects of MST affected the views of themselves or of the world	"It really messed with my ability to trust."
Long wait for appointments/support	Difficulties they encountered with the mental health system when attempting to begin or continue their services	"it just seems like unless someone is going to literally commit suicide, it seems really impossible to get quick support."
Positively affected wellbeing	How the mental health treatment affected their ongoing well-being	"It allowed me to be more functional and cope with things."

Positively affected Quality of Life (QoL)	How mental health treatment affected their ongoing QoL	"I think having that stable relationship helps. Every week having somebody there, because there are things that I talk about with them that I can't talk about with anyone else."

Thematic Analysis. Once inductive reasoning was used to identify codes, thematic analysis was applied. Thematic analysis is important because it is the researcher's method to identify, analyze, and interpret the themes from the data set

(Christou, 2023). "The Coding Manual for Qualitative Researchers" (2021) by Saldaña guided the manual coding process. After the transcripts were transcribed and checked, thematic analysis was used to identify and generate the codes, create categories, develop high-level categories, and identify and apply the emerging themes.

QOLS Analysis. The QOLS survey was given through Survey Monkey©. The participants answered the questions based on their feelings about certain areas of their QoL and well-being based on the outcomes of the mental health support and services they either received or are still receiving. The results were mainly mixed in the 16 areas of analysis for the QOLS, meaning the majority of the participants were neither satisfied nor dissatisfied in the areas of QoL and well-being based on the care they received. The QOLS was a good introduction to the interviews. In the interviews, the participants were able to expand upon the survey results to obtain more clear and concise information regarding mental health care and the participants' QoL and well-being.

Table 7

Quality of Life Survey (QOLS) Responses

QoL Area	Terrible	Unhappy	Mostly dissatis.	Mixed	Mostly satisf.	Pleased	Delighted
materials, comforts, home, food conveniences, financial security	0 (0%)	0 (0%)	4 (20%)	6 (30%)	6 (30%)	4 (20%)	0 (0%)
health - being physically fit & vigorous	2 (10%)	3 (15%)	4 (20%)	7 (35%)	4 (20%)	0 (0%)	0 (0%)
Relationships with parents, siblings, & other relatives	2 (10%)	2 (10%)	2 (10%)	5 (25%)	6 (30%)	2 (10%)	1 (5%)
Having & rearing children	2 (10%)	1 (5%)	1 (5%)	6 (30%)	4 (20%)	3 (15%)	3 (15%)
Close relationship with spouse or significant other	4 (20%)	2 (10%)	1 (5%)	4 (20%)	5 (20%)	3 (15%)	1 (5%)
Close friends	0 (0%)	2 (10%)	2 (10%)	6 (30%)	3 (15%)	5 (25%)	2 (10%)
Helping & encouraging others, volunteering, giving advice	0 (0%)	0 (0%)	0 (0%)	5 (25%)	2 (10%)	7 (35%)	6 (30%)
Participating in organizations & public affairs	1 (5%)	0 (0%)	1 (5%)	6 (30%)	2 (10%)	6 (30%)	4 (20%)
Learning - attending school, improving understanding, getting additional knowledge	0 (0%)	0 (0%)	1 (5%)	5 (25%)	4 (20%)	5 (25%)	5 (25%)
Understanding yourself	0 (0%)	1 (5%)	0 (0%)	9 (45%)	2 (10%)	6 (30%)	2 (10%)
Work - job or in home	2 (10%)	0 (0%)	1 (5%)	6 (30%)	5 (25%)	6 (30%)	0 (0%)

Expressing yourself creatively	1 (5%)	1 (5%)	4 (20%)	2 (10%)	6 (30%)	6 (30%)	0 (0%)
Socializing - meeting other people, doing things, parties, etc.	0 (0%)	2 (10%)	4 (20%)	7 (35%)	4 (20%)	3 (15%)	0 (0%)
Reading, listening to music, or observing entertainment	0 (0%)	0 (0%)	1 (5%)	5 (25%)	4 (20%)	8 (40%)	2 (10%)
Participating in active recreation	0 (0%)	3 (15%)	1 (5%)	8 (40%)	5 (25%)	3 (15%)	0 (0%)
Independence, doing for yourself	0 (0%)	0 (0%)	2 (10%)	9 (45%)	1 (5%)	6(30%)	2 (10%)

Coding the Interviews. The coding process began after this researcher became familiar with the data collected by reviewing the transcripts several times. This was achieved by listening to the audio recordings of the interviews and reading through the transcripts repeatedly to ensure familiarization with the information (Khokar et al., 2020). While listening to the audio recordings, I added to my notes taken during the interview related to inflections in tone of voice, laughing, pauses, and sniffling. The review of this information assisted this researcher in understanding the participants' responses to specific questions.

At the beginning of each participant interview, participant codes were assigned (P1-P12). These codes were utilized throughout the coding process. RQ1 and RQ2 were noted on separate post-it notes so that this researcher could easily access the information while looking for codes and themes throughout the 12 participant interview transcripts. For the first step of thematic analysis, I began manually coding the interviews by printing each on paper and reviewing them using different-colored markers to identify similar and different codes. After identifying over 10 different codes, this researcher acknowledged that it was difficult to keep them separate because the colors had to be utilized several times. After further researching additional information about manual coding, I downloaded MAXQDA and continued manual coding through this program.

This researcher uploaded each interview transcript to MAXQDA for manual coding. After this step, I began reviewing the individual transcripts again. The transcripts were manually coded, and each code was assigned a color. Although each color was utilized more than once in MAXQDA, the difference was that the MAXQDA program could organize the information more clearly than manually coding through each transcript on paper. This step in the process aligned with Yin's pattern-matching.

Repeated words, phrases, and ideas were identified through analysis of the transcribed data. In this stage of manual coding, it was important to ensure that equal attention was given to each data set (Christou, 2023). Some codes were utilized in more than one data set because they could mean more than one thing within the context of the interviews. For example, "provider cancellations" was something that the participants said when talking about their mental health providers but also when talking about waiting for their mental health care. Identifying and utilizing the most frequent codes within the data helped identify the themes (Rogers, 2018).

In the next step, this researcher searched for themes that emerged from within the coded data. In this process, I reviewed the coded data and grouped it into similar categories to begin developing the themes. Using Yin's pattern matching to color code the data helped to better group information and search for emerging themes.

Special attention was given to the codes collected concerning Maslow's Hierarchy of Needs (Maslow, 1943, 1954) and Deci and Ryan's self-determination theory (1985a). How participants explained the mental health services and support they received and how it affected specific areas in their lives was important to understand when grouping the codes into categories in preparation for assigning themes to the data (See Figure 7). Refining the collected information was an important part of this process. It allowed some items to be rearranged and or regrouped to ensure they continued aligning with the forming themes (Christou, 2023). For example, P11 stated it was "impossible to get quick support," and P1 stated, "6 months it's a long wait for anything." These codes were grouped in the theme of long wait times for appointments.

Figure 7

Maslow's Hierarchy of Needs and Self-Determination Theory in the Interviews

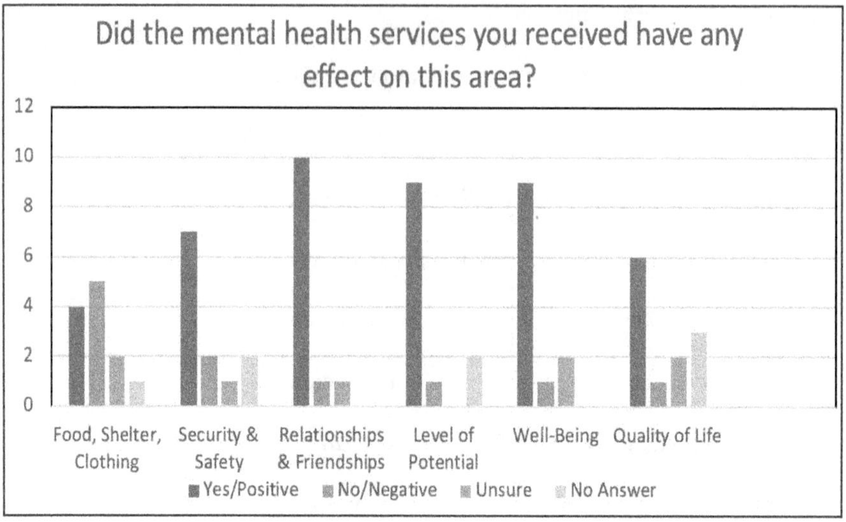

The last step in the process was important when naming the themes to ensure they represented the information collected (Christou, 2023). When naming the themes, this researcher identified what each theme told about the data collected (Maguire & Delahunt, 2017). The themes that emerged told a story about how the female veterans experienced mental health services and support for MST and how it affected their QoL and wellbeing. The emerging themes told of negative and positive experiences and overall increased well-being and QoL with the services and support. Ensuring that the themes aligned with the research questions and problem statement was an important aspect of this step of the thematic analysis process (Christou, 2023).

In this step, this researcher examined each group of categories and applied them to RQ1 and RQ2. The high-level categories were identified, analyzed, and combined to accurately interpret the participants' experiences with mental health services and their QoL and well-being. The first theme defined in RQ1 was "female veterans described long wait times as difficulties with their mental health care after discharge." This theme was synthesized from high-level categories that addressed:

(a) referrals to the wrong service

(b) shortage of providers

(c) suicidal patients get priority

The second theme identified in RQ2 was "female veterans described having a supportive mental health provider as a positive experience after discharge." These themes were generated from high-level categories that addressed:

(a) non-judgmental of their level of need

(b) not feeling pressured

(c) providing options for care

(d) the honesty of the provider

RQ2's theme, "once engaged, mental health services and support contributed to a positive quality of life and well-being, increasing life functioning and stability," was synthesized from high-level categories that addressed:

(a) increased sense of safety

(b) feelings of belongingness and love

(c) feeling more powerful

(d) increased potential (e) getting needs met.

The final report is the culmination of information broken down and thoroughly explained in this book. The goal is to explain the validity of the data analysis with sufficient evidence to connect the themes to the data collected (Christou, 2023). The most important part is to ensure that the theories accurately represent the voices of the research participants. The inductive analysis supported me in achieving this goal. RQ1 presented two themes, and RQ2 presented one.

Coding the Reflection Journal. Only one reflection journal was returned to this researcher. The reflection journal was uploaded to MAXQDA for manual coding. As completed in the interview coding process, this researcher read through the reflection journal to identify codes, categories, and high-level categories that were noted in the journal. P7 further expanded upon the difficulties of obtaining services for MST after discharge. Participant 7 explained the difficulties of even talking about the MST to be able to report it while enlisted, but also, as a veteran, it can present as a large barrier to seeking the services needed after discharge. P7 indicated that the barrier to care is having to speak about it to receive services after being conditioned in the military not to speak about the assault, so many female veterans go without the option of care because of this difficulty.

Table 8

Research Questions and Identified Themes

Research Question	Themes

RQ1: How do female veterans of MST describe their experiences with mental health care services after discharge?	Female veterans described long wait times as difficulties with their experiences with mental health care after discharge; Female veterans described having a supportive mental health provider as a positive experience after discharge
RQ2: How do female veteran survivors of military sexual trauma describe the effects of post-military mental health care services on their quality of life and well-being?	Once engaged, mental health services and support contributed to a positive well-being and quality of life, increasing life functioning and stability

Results

Presenting the Results

This section will present the results of this qualitative descriptive study. It will provide information about the data and the analysis of that data. The outcome of the reflexivity protocol will be addressed and explained to address the potential biases present in the study. The research questions and themes will be presented and explained, along with the identified codes.

Reflexivity Protocol Outcome. The reflexivity process was utilized from the research beginning to collecting, analyzing, and presenting data. Before beginning the data collection, this researcher explored two areas that could create bias and influence the process. The first was that I am a licensed clinical social worker and therapist who works with veterans daily, most of them with some type of trauma. The second was that I am also an Army veteran who served from 2001-2003 and was cognizant of MST occurring within the unit of assignment. These life experiences could influence a researcher's outlook and the study. Several checks were implemented to ensure reflexivity throughout the process.

The first check ensured awareness of the areas of bias and personal opinion and kept them at the forefront throughout the process. The second check was to reflect on each interview once completed to critique if there was any personal opinion or bias. It was helpful to review the interview audio recordings and listen to how this researcher replied or acknowledged some of the answers provided by the participants. The third check was to make notes of anything that was noticed and review it before the beginning of the next participant interview. The three-step process was helpful and a positive addition to the research process.

Research Questions and Themes: Analysis Results. The goal of this qualitative descriptive study was to explore how female military survivors of active-duty military sexual trauma would describe the effects of their post-military provided mental health care on their quality of life and well-being (Brown et al., 2021; Calhoun et al., 2018; Holland et al., 2016; Kintzle et al., 2015; Matt et al., 2020; Starzynski et al., 2017). A qualitative methodology was selected because it allowed the research participants to share their feelings, beliefs, and thoughts related to the topic (Delgado-Hito & RomeroGarcia, 2021), allowing for themes and trends to be uncovered within the data (Park & Park, 2016). A descriptive design was selected because it gave a detailed description of areas such as who was involved, what was involved, and the things involved, directly from the individual who lived through that experience (Lambert & Lambert, 2012; West et al., 2017).

The phenomenon studied was how mental health services after MST that occurred while on active duty contributed to the female veterans' QoL and well-being after discharge from the military. Hendrikx et al., 2021 explained that MST can make it more difficult for individuals to achieve well-being during enlistment and after discharge.

Williams et al., 2017 explained that MST survivors are likelier to experience diminished QoL. The research questions, Maslow's Hierarchy of Needs Theory (1943, 1954), and Deci and Ryan's self-determination theory (1985a) guided the research and analyzed the phenomenon.

The study utilized two research questions to understand the phenomenon. The first research question sought to understand the experiences the female veterans had with mental health care. The second research question sought to understand how those resources utilized in research question one either positively or negatively affected their QoL and well-being. The research questions that guided the study were:

RQ1: How do female veteran survivors of military sexual trauma describe their experiences with mental health care services after discharge?

RQ2: How do female veteran survivors of military sexual trauma describe the effects of post-military mental health care services on their quality of life and well-being?

Three sources of information to explore the research questions: the quality-of-life questionnaire (see Appendix G), semi-structured open-ended interviews, and a reflection journal (see Appendix M). To analyze the sources, inductive reasoning was utilized to identify codes, and thematic analysis was applied to identify themes that emerged from the data. Several rounds of coding were completed before grouping the codes into categories, high-level categories, and themes. The themes that emerged were the themes that answered the two research questions according to the female veteran participants.

Research Question 1

How do female veterans of MST describe their experiences with mental health care services after discharge? This research question was essential to understand the experiences that the research participants had while receiving mental health care as veterans. The female veterans shared their experiences seeking and then engaging in mental health services. The participants explained that the services they sought were not solely within the VA but also through private providers, VA referrals, and other community resources. Long wait times plagued these veterans in trying to seek services for their immediate symptoms. The delay in treatment resulted in an exacerbation of mental health symptoms and a distrust in the system meant to treat its nation's veterans. The participants also shared that once engaged in services with a supportive mental health professional, their experience with veteran's mental health care services, whether public or private, was a positive experience.

Theme 1: Female Veterans Described Long Wait Times as Difficulties with Their Experiences with Mental Health Care After Discharge. Female veterans seek mental health support for MST through many different resources, such as the Veteran's Administration (VA), their own private medical insurance, community providers, and other private and public providers, as well as for-profit and non-profit organizations. This theme is related to how the female veterans shared their personal experiences with seeking and engaging in mental health care for MST support. In the study, participants shared their experiences with long wait times to either begin services or to switch between services. Only a couple of veterans described a smooth transition from military mental health care while enlisted to veteran mental health care after discharge. These instances came when their active-duty provider referred them directly to their civilian mental health provider. Still, most shared their engagement difficulties (see Table 9). The effects of the long wait time included an exacerbation of the mental health symptoms, as well as a decrease in their trust in the veteran's health systems (both public and private).

Table 9

Long Wait Times for Mental Health Care After Discharge

Participant	Comments
P1	"If I get rescheduled for something, it's like six months out, it's a very long wait for anything, and that is a little bit frustrating."
P4	"It took at least four or five months to get that care to begin with."
P5	"VA referred me out to a community provider, so that probably took three or four months to get on their books."
P11	"Just seems unless someone's literally gonna, like, commit suicide, it seems really impossible to get quick support."

Exacerbation of Mental Health Symptoms. The veterans explained that the long wait times exacerbated their mental health symptoms. PTSD symptoms, such as nightmares, flashbacks, depression, hypervigilance, chronic pain, and anxiety, increased during the waiting time for the initial appointment and or during the wait for the referral to other services. P4 stated, "They told me the next appointment was January, February, I needed medication… I was failing at life, I was suffering, and it wasn't fair." Many veterans felt as though they had to take the care and management of their symptoms into their own hands. Sometimes, checking themselves into a mental health facility, use or abuse substances to cope with mental health symptoms, or engage in other risk-taking behaviors. P5 shared, "I think it drove behavior where I was trying to treat myself. It kind of makes you lose hope and it's easy to give up." Some of the participants who are not currently engaged in mental health care stated that it was due to the wait time and the exacerbation of their mental health symptoms; They felt forgotten.

Decreased Their Trust in The Veteran's Health Systems. The frustration of serving their country and then having such a lengthy delay in service when they needed it was a shared sentiment. In April 2014, there were national media stories released about the wait time for veteran care services, which led to a decreased trust in these systems, noting that some veterans die just waiting for care (Jones et al., 2021). P3 shared, "One of the barriers to receiving care is experience. By the terrible experience, the odds of coming back are reduced significantly and the more bad experiences you have had, the less. Most of the service members that are dying by suicide do not receive care. The barriers to treatment shouldn't be there." The veterans shared that putting their trust in a system that lets them down greatly decreases their trust in returning to care.

Theme 2: Female Veterans Described Having a Supportive Mental Health Provider as a Positive Experience After Discharge. The participants receive their mental health care services from various mental health providers such as psychiatrists, psychologists, licensed clinical social workers (LCSWs), marriage and family therapists (MFTs), and licensed professional counselors (LPCs). Although these providers may have provided a different level of care, the positive experiences that the veterans had with them were important to setting the tone of their ongoing mental health care for their symptoms. The veterans who shared their positive experiences with their mental health providers explained that their provider involving them in decisions about their care was an important aspect, as well as feeling that they were supported and were being listened to. Building rapport and having a safe space has been integral in their ongoing trust and treatment engagement (see Table 10).

Table 10

Theme 2: Having a Supportive Mental Health Provider as a Positive Experience

Participant	Comments
P8	"the psychiatrist and the psychologist, they would try to force me to talk about it, and that would cause me to disassociate. And I finally, switched and I got a, actually a social worker, who refused to make, make me talk about it. We talked round about, like, family life, what was it like for me? You know, just symptoms, what I was going through on a daily basis, and not the actual core, the roots. And the therapist actually discussed with me about different types of therapies like cognitive behavioral."

P9	"And the opportunity to change providers if I didn't click with them was also very appreciated, too. They made that very clear. Like, please don't feel like you just have to get stuck with me if we're not clicking or you're not comfortable. All you have to do is just like, all you have to do is tell me. You don't even have to tell me. You can tell my boss, and I will not be I won't even know. And you know, like, I think even just saying that makes me more willing to communicate and open up a little bit too, like, it just kind of sets the stage on a good foot."
P12	"When I went in and said, I am [expletive] up. I need help right now; I was immediately into the system and got set up with a wonderful psychiatrist. He was amazing and totally available to me, like I felt like I was his number one priority, yeah, you know, like I was in that kind of thinking. So, I did have immediate access to a psychiatrist."

Being Involved in Decisions about Their Mental Health Care. The veterans who felt that their mental health care provider involved them in the decisions about their mental health care and treatment decisions had a positive experience. Marsh et al. (2012) explained that the client-provider working alliance is important and builds a therapeutic relationship when both can work together to identify goals for therapy, therapy tasks, and the relationship bond. P8 shared that she felt her initial mental health providers tried to force her into treatments that were not conducive for her at the time. Once she was able to switch providers, and that provider listened to her and ensured that she was involved in her care, she began feeling more positive and engaged in the mental health treatment she was given. When these bonds are built, they help to facilitate therapeutic interventions (Marsh et al., 2012).

Feeling Supported and Listened To. Not only is it important to feel involved in their mental health care, but feeling supported and listened to was an important aspect shared by the female veteran participants. P8 shared about her current mental health provider, stating, "He actually really cares and listens, and he'll talk, and I'll talk, and then if I kind of go off, he doesn't have a script like most of them do. He reads me and that's the true treatment." Feeling listened to develops a healthy relationship between the client and the provider. When the client feels listened to and like they can discuss more than just their problems, this helps to form a more positive relationship and is a vital aspect of the healing process (Borg & Kristiansen, 2004).

Research Question 1 Conclusion. Female veterans of military sexual trauma described their experiences with mental health care services after discharge as both positive and negative. The negative aspects focused on the wait times to receive the care, which resulted in an exacerbation of mental health symptoms and a loss of trust in the veteran's mental health care system. The more positive aspect focused on having a supportive mental health care provider once the care was begun. It is important to understand that not everyone can try again after a negative experience, so having that positive engagement with the first contact is extremely important.

Wang et al. (2007) emphasized the importance of providing mental health services and support earlier in the process to mitigate the negative consequences of the delay in service. Unfortunately, these veterans experienced a delay in their mental health care services in treatment of the effects of the MST they endured. Due to the lack of available resources and the timely scheduling of mental health care, their symptoms were exacerbated, causing other difficulties and mistrust. They shared that a negative experience makes it almost difficult to return, making it imperative to ensure these interactions are positive from the beginning.

Thompson and McCabe (2012) explained that the working alliance between patient and provider is important to improve positive outcomes and engagement. The authors mentioned that when the patient feels engaged and supported by their mental health provider, they feel like their care is more collaborative, thus creating a more positive experience. The participants shared that the providers that have engaged them in their care and made them feel a part of their treatment decisions have been the most helpful. Developing a healthy relationship is integral to this process. The female veterans who were included in their care decisions and felt like they had a safe space to express themselves with their mental health provider had more positive outcomes with their mental health care, thus increasing their positive mental health outcomes with QoL and well-being.

Research Question 2

How do female veteran survivors of military sexual trauma describe the effects of post-military mental health care services on their quality of life and well-being? This research question is important to understand how the services and support received affected the veteran's quality of life and well-being. The veterans shared their positive and negative experiences and how these experiences contributed to their ongoing QoL and well-being.

Theme 1: Once Engaged, Mental Health Services and Support Contributed to a Positive Quality of Life and Well-being, Increasing Life Functioning and

Stability. The QOLS and interviews revealed more positive well-being and QoL effects with the services and support received. Most participants shared that mental health services and support have had a positive impact on their QoL and well-being, increasing their sense of hedonia and eudaimonia. They shared aspects of their potential that have improved and how they are working toward fulfilling their personal needs (see Table 11). Positive interactions with their mental health care provider, setting goals for their interactions, and developing the skills needed to improve their lives continually are important in contributing to positive well-being and QoL (Gigantesco & Giuliani, 2011).

Table 11

Positive Effects on QoL and Well-being

Participant	Comments
P6	"Treatment positively affected my well-being when I got the right counselor."
P7	"I used to hear very negative thoughts, now I counter it."
P8	"I learned the skills to cope when it gets too much."
P9	"I think it [mental health care] really impacted every part of my life in mostly good ways."

Feeling an Increase in Their Potential. The participants explained that their level of potential increased due to the mental health care services and support received. P9 stated, "I definitely have a more strong sense of myself and my value system." P7 stated, "It helped me maintain kind of status quo on my sanity." Potential is an aspect of eudaimonia and increases a person's positive psychological health (Cooke et al., 2016; Disabato et al., 2016). The most important impact in this area that was shared was the skills learned, which allowed them to take their lives back into their own hands. Some shared that their MST experience left them feeling powerless. However, the positive mental health care services and support received allowed them to take that power back again and feel in control of themselves while utilizing the new coping skills and strategies learned.

Positive Needs Fulfillment. Hedonia focuses on a positive sense of life (Cooke et al., 2016). The participants shared that when their needs are fulfilled in several areas of their lives, it increases their QoL and well-being. Areas such as security and safety, relationships and friendships, and self-esteem, when fulfilled positively, create a positive sense of life. P10 stated, "Creating that space in me to be able to take care of myself, make myself a priority" has been something that has helped her positively from the mental health care that she received. P7 talked about "deliberate mindfulness" when engaging in mental health care, contributing to a positive QoL and well-being in her life. In Maslow's hierarchy of needs, needs fulfillment is integral to moving through the stages of self-actualization and or intrinsic values (Sirgy, 1986).

Limitations

The limitations presented in this qualitative descriptive study are as follows:

1. Participants' self-report: Considering the sensitive nature of the study, participants are usually hesitant to disclose sensitive information, which can affect the study's data collection (Pickard et al., 2018). The

topic of the study asked participants to provide information about the services and support they received after experiencing MST. Although the study did not specifically ask for details about their MST experience, it is important to understand that the experience may be recalled and lead to some hesitation or holding back information about what is being asked (Pickard et al., 2018).

2. The researcher's own bias: I was acutely aware of possible personal biases, and to mitigate the possibility of this limitation, I did self-reflection before and after the interviews. Journaling was utilized and often revisited during data collection and analysis. The reflexivity protocol section in Chapter 4 provides a detailed explanation of this process.

Transferability

Transferability refers to how the data obtained from one study can also be applicable in other settings (Lemon & Hayes, 2020). This study's descriptive details, including direct quotes, visual observations, and emotional cues, help to provide a thick description, thus increasing the possibility of transferability within this study (Lim, 2024). Thick description makes the findings more relatable because it paints a picture of the process through its informative explanation of the research processes (Lim, 2024). This study provided rich detail about the study population, why that study was chosen, how they were chosen, and from where they were chosen. The research process of collecting the QOLS, completing the individual interviews, and the reflection journal process were outlined with specifics about each process. The results were presented with direct quotations, explanations, and charts to provide a visual of the process.

Transferability is possible, and other researchers can build upon or replicate this process, if desired.

Summary

The purpose of this qualitative descriptive study was to understand how female military survivors of active-duty military sexual trauma who reside within the United States would describe the effects of their post-military provided mental health care services on their quality of life and well-being. The two research questions for this study were presented and answered:

RQ1: How do female veteran survivors of military sexual trauma describe their experiences with mental health care services after discharge?

RQ2: How do female veteran survivors of military sexual trauma describe the effects of post-military mental health care services on their quality of life and well-being?

The three data sources for this study included an online delivery of the quality-of-life questionnaire (see Appendix G)), audio-recorded semi-structured individual interviews, and a reflection journal (see Appendix M).

Chapter 4 described and presented the information obtained for this study to answer the research questions. It was found that female veterans of MST feel that the long wait times for veteran mental health care are a negative aspect of their care.

However, once they can receive care from a supportive mental health professional, their QoL and well-being will increase. Chapter 5 provides the summary, conclusions, and

recommendations of the study.

Chapter 5: Summary, Conclusions, and Recommendations

Introduction and Summary of Study

Military sexual trauma is defined as sexual assault and or sexual harassment experienced by active-duty women or men while serving in active-duty training, inactive training, or otherwise on active duty in any capacity, position, or rank (Monteith et al., 2019; U.S. Department of Veterans Affairs, 2023) and it has been a problem since at least World War II (Valente & Wight, 2007). Although it has been a problem in the military for several years, there have not been many studies about the effects of MST and how the services and support affect the survivors (Cole et al., 2022; Holland et al., 2016; Kintzle et al., 2015; Reinhardt et al., 2023). Previous studies concluded that it was important to identify which facet of care offers the most benefit to veteran survivors of MST (Matt et al., 2020). This study was designed and executed to contribute to the body of knowledge in this area.

Considering the limited knowledge and information in this area, this study attempted to add to the literature by conducting a study that directly addressed the gap in the literature. This qualitative descriptive study examined how the effects of mental health services and support after military sexual trauma (MST) affected female veterans' quality of life and well-being. A qualitative methodology was used to examine the perspectives of the female survivors of MST. A descriptive study supported the participants in explaining their everyday experiences (Lambert & Lambert, 2012). It helped me to analyze the effects of the services and support on their QoL and well-being.

This chapter will explain this information further.

Chapter 5 will begin with an overview of why the study was important and how it contributed to the body of knowledge regarding MST, services and support, and QoL and well-being. A summary of the findings and a conclusion will be discussed, reflecting on the process of this book. Theoretical implications, practical implications, future research implications, and the strengths and weaknesses of the study will be outlined. To conclude Chapter 5, recommendations for further research, future practice, and a holistic reflection on the problem space will be addressed.

Summary of Findings and Conclusion

Overall Organization

The study's targeted sample were female veteran survivors of MST who resided in the United States of America and who received mental health care services and support for that trauma in 2004 or after. The study focused on 2004 or after for mental health services and support because that was the year that the Sexual Assault Prevention and Response Office (SAPRO) was formed (Gonzalez-Prats, 2017). The sample of this study was directly recruited from this population.

The study utilized three data collection tools: a QoL survey, semi-structured openended interviews, and a reflection journal. Twenty female veterans completed the QoL survey, which was conducted via Survey Monkey©. Twelve participants completed the semi-structured open-ended interviews, which were scheduled at their leisure and completed via the online Zoom platform with this researcher. One participant returned the reflection journal, which was emailed back after member-checking was completed on their interview transcript.

The problem statement that led this study was that it was not known how female military survivors of active-duty military sexual trauma will describe the effects of their post-military provided mental health care on their quality of life (QoL) and well-being. The theorics that led this study were Maslow's Hierarchy of Needs (1943, 1954) and Deci and Ryan's self-determination theory (1985a). The research questions developed for this study were:

RQ1: How do female veteran survivors of military sexual trauma describe their experiences with mental health care services after discharge?

RQ2: How do female veteran survivors of military sexual trauma describe the effects of post-military mental health care services on their quality of life and well-being?

The three data collection methods assisted with guiding this research and applying the collected information to the research questions. The information was analyzed and triangulated to apply to the research questions. Chapter 4 provided several tables and graphs showing and explaining how the data was collected, analyzed, and organized.

With that information, themes were identified.

Research Question 1

This research question examined the experiences that the participants had with the mental health care services that they received as veterans after their discharge from the military. The findings indicated that the participants had varying positive and negative experiences but also shared similar experiences. The participants were able to identify experiences that helped them seek services and support, as well as things that were not helpful; some identifying things that have deterred them from returning to services and support for their MST experience.

The participants shared examples of positive experiences with mental health care services after discharge, such as having a supportive mental health care provider. Some indicators of positive experiences with supportive mental health service providers involved having good interactions with the veteran's crisis line, receiving guidance from their provider about the services and support that would be most helpful for them, and getting familiarized with the Veteran's Affairs (VA). The veteran's crisis line interactions were directly related to obtaining a prompt initial mental health service appointment.

Participants also shared examples of negative experiences with mental health care services after discharge, such as having long wait times for appointments, not having a good connection with their mental health provider and experiencing sexual harassment while receiving care at a veterans mental health facility. Some of the indicators of having long waits for mental health care appointments were associated with the facilities being short-staffed, difficulties with receiving referrals for appropriate services, and the femalespecific care being too far from the veteran's residence. The main reasons participants felt a disconnect from their mental health providers were that some of them were assigned a male provider, they felt their male mental health provider had a lack of training and was unable to handle the level of mental health care that they needed, and or they felt their provider pushed them too far for care they were not ready to participate in the type of care suggested.

Overall, two themes emerged from the data collected about research question one.

The first theme was that female veterans described having long wait times as difficulties with their experiences with mental health care after discharge. The second theme was that female veterans described having a supportive mental health provider as a positive experience after discharge.

Research Question 2

This research question examined how the participants felt their QoL, and wellbeing were affected by the mental health care services that they received. The findings indicated that the participants' QoL and well-being were more positively impacted by the services and support received than negatively affected. They identified the areas of care that directly contributed to a higher QoL and well-being in self-actualization, esteem, belongingness and love, safety and security, and physiological needs. Hedonia and eudaimonia were also taken into account.

Hedonia was examined as the participants' self-appraisal of how satisfied they are with their lives, possessing a positive effect and the absence of an adverse impact (Mise & Busseri, 2020) directly related to the services and support received. Similarly, eudaimonia was examined as how the participants viewed their growth and flourishing as humans while living up to their full potential in self-growth and self-actualization (Disabato et al., 2016; Rahmani et al., 2018). The participants were asked directly and indirectly about these areas in their lives and how they related to the services and support they have received thus far. The theme that emerged from the data was that once engaged, mental health services and support contributed to a positive QoL and wellbeing, increasing life functioning and stability.

Some examples of the specific services and support that the participants shared that positively affected their QoL and well-being were specific therapies, programs, and skills learned. Some of the particular therapies that the participants shared as being the most helpful included cognitive behavioral therapy (CBT), cognitive processing therapy (CPT), eye movement and desensitization reprocessing therapy (EMDR), and dialectical behavioral therapy (DBT), citing changes in their thought processes as the key to positive care. Specific coping skills that have been helpful for them include different breathing techniques, journaling, mindfulness, and meditation. Most participants either are still participating in the mental health care services and support or have continued to utilize the coping skills they learned while in treatment.

It is important to understand that while data saturation was achieved early in the study process, some veterans reported extremely negative experiences with the services and support they received, thus leading to no engagement in services to address the MST they experienced. These veterans explained that the disconnect in obtaining an appointment or constantly being assigned to a mental health provider who was not empathetic or helpful with their specific process was damaging to their faith in the veteran's mental health system. Unfortunately, their QoL and well-being have not improved, and they have been left with trying to find ways to cope and navigate through civilian life as a survivor of MST alone.

Reflection on the book Process

The book process was a learning experience for this researcher. When entering this doctoral program, there were many misconceptions about the research process and many personal difficulties that presented themselves along the way. This researcher learned that the doctoral program requires a different level of grit and thinking than the previous Bachelor's and Master's programs. Beginning this process several years ago, knowing little about research, and then getting to the end as someone who understands research applications and processes is an accomplishment.

Many things along the way added to the difficulty of completing this process promptly. Being a wife and mother has always been the priority, but juggling working two jobs, taking care of family members, and practicing the self-care I teach my regular clients as their mental health therapist was more difficult throughout this process. Also, in the middle of this program, the COVID-19 pandemic took over everyday life. Working from home for both jobs, homeschooling the children, and managing to keep the family safe, on top of writing a book, proved to be one of the most difficult things this researcher had to juggle.

The reflexivity protocol was an important and helpful tool to support this researcher in remaining vigilant about any biases or things that could affect the research process. This was helpful to use and understand because, as a military veteran, a mental health therapist, and a therapist who treats veterans who have experienced trauma, it is easy to overlook the bias when it involves daily interactions and life experiences. Besides learning about research and being able to apply those concepts, the reflexivity protocol was one of the most important tools overall.

When this researcher began completing the surveys and talking to several female veterans, it was eye-opening to learn about our female veterans' lack of services. This researcher received several phone calls from other female veterans who wanted to express their support in the study but were not ready to participate or they served in the military before 2004. The solidarity between our nation's female veterans and their desire to want to help another female veteran out was positively overwhelming.

Implications

The literature review in Chapter 2 helped this researcher to identify a problem space about MST services and support as they relate to a veteran's QoL and well-being. Chapter 2 and the literature review concluded that further information was needed to understand which facets of care were needed to provide the most benefit after MST (Matt et al., 2020). Survivors of sexual trauma are at greater risk for decreased well-being and QoL (Vogt et

al., 2021; Williams et al., 2017). Their mental health is affected, thus contributing to adverse mental and physical health outcomes such as increased suicide risk, posttraumatic stress disorder (PTSD), depression, anxiety, chronic pain, obesity, sexual dysfunction, and substance abuse (Kelly, 2021; Preston et al., 2022; U.S.
Department of Veterans Affairs, 2023).

Learning about the experiences of female veteran survivors of MST and their outcomes from the services and support they received directly from those who have experienced them is the key to changing future outcomes. This research added to the body of knowledge already out there but also provided new perspectives on what benefits this population. The research was focused on describing and explaining the phenomena in the natural setting of those who experienced them (Draper, 2004).

Theoretical Implications

The theories applied to this qualitative descriptive study were Maslow's
Hierarchy of Needs (1943, 1954) and Deci and Ryan's (1985a) self-determination theory. Maslow's (1943, 1954) motivational theory focuses on feeling safe before accomplishing other human needs. Extreme stress or trauma are instances that can negatively affect progress and create a barrier unless treated effectively (N. Parker, 2021). Selfdetermination theory describes motivation and identifies resilience as positively affecting QoL and well-being. The higher the level of support, the more positive contributions to self-determination (Perlman et al., 2018). If the treatment setting is positive,

it will most likely positively affect motivation, thus increasing the chances of a more positive outcome (Mancini, 2008).

Participants in this study indicated that the positive interactions they encountered with their mental health providers led to better engagement, increased coping skills, and good rapport in building trust. Many participants acknowledged the difficulties with obtaining effective mental health services for MST. Still, once they were placed in the right supportive care environment, they felt more motivated to improve their QoL and well-being. The effective mental health services they received assisted with feeling a sense of safety in their life to begin to focus on the MST and its effects. It is important to note that the participants who have not encountered positive mental health services and support outcomes continue to struggle in areas of mental health as it relates to quality of life, well-being, and self-determination ideas.

Applying Maslow's Hierarchy of Needs and Deci and Ryan's Self-Determination

Theory helped this research highlight the importance of mental health care for female MST survivors. Participants were explicitly asked about how their mental health care affected their quality of life and well-being in the areas of Maslow's Hierarchy of Needs and self-determination theory: (a) food, shelter, clothing, (b) security and safety, (c) relationships and friendships, (d) level of potential, (e) well-being, and (f) quality of life. Figure 7 broke down how many participants indicated a positive effect, a negative effect, unsure, or no answer. The QOLS also addressed 16 areas of quality of life and wellbeing, and the participants could answer whether the services were helpful in those areas. The information concluded that the importance of needs fulfillment in several areas of life is to be able to have a positive mental health outcome.

Practical Implications

As highlighted previously, past studies focused on active-duty women in the military and women veterans who experienced MST and how their experience related to suicidal ideation and or attempted suicide, their exposure to combat, and or their history of childhood sexual assault (CSA; Baca et al., 2021; Bosch et al., 2020; Gross et al., 2019; Holliday et al., 2023; Monteith et al., 2019). Previous studies did not specifically focus on how female veterans with a history of MST perceived the effect(s) of military mental health services they received while on active duty, their post-active-duty mental health services, and how those services may or may not have contributed to their wellbeing and quality of life post-military service (Reinhardt et al., 2023).

The findings of this study can be applied to many practical implications when determining best practices in support of female veterans who are survivors of MST. One of the most significant implications was understanding the supportive needs of female veterans to support their engagement in mental health services for the effects of MST. For example, female veterans shared that being connected to mental health services directly from their military enlistment helped with continuity of care. This aspect of continuity of care may have future implications in decreasing the wait time for mental health care once discharged from the military. The participants shared that the long wait times affected their mental health and decreased their QoL and well-being. In contrast, getting sooner care could increase QoL and well-being for our veterans after MST.

Understanding these interpretations can help explicate programs and services to create a bridge to ensure continuity of care and shorter wait times.

A positive connection with their mental health care provider and fulfilling needs also contributed to the female veterans' positive quality of life and well-being. They shared that being treated by a mental health provider who was not well-equipped to handle their mental health needs was detrimental to their progress. This barrier to effective care may affect progress in Maslow's Hierarchy of Needs or Deci and Ryan's self-determination theory (1985a). Understanding this aspect can have future practical implications. Ensuring that mental health providers who are treating veterans with MST are well-trained to support this population. This study can guide future practices to determine the level of need for this veteran population and staff veteran healthcare facilities in a way that can align with the needs of this population.

Future Research Implications

This study addressed the problem space of the literature, focusing on the effects of post-military provided mental health care on the quality of life and well-being of female veteran survivors of MST. Although more research needs to be conducted, it provides the groundwork and the direction for possible future research. Since the study did not obtain input from all six military branches, it would be essential for future research to obtain more well-rounded information. This study did not include any male veterans, only female veterans. It is important to understand that female veterans experience MST at alarming rates, but male veterans have also experienced the trauma and are survivors of MST. It is suggested that future research include male veteran survivors of MST to understand their experiences with mental health care services and support as veterans after MST. It is also recommended that future research utilize other data collection procedures to obtain more well-rounded information. Focus groups are another effective form of data collection that could benefit this area. Sometimes, when members of a focus group feel supported, more information will be shared, thus contributing to a larger body of information to be analyzed on the topic and contributing to group reflexivity (Freeman, 2006).

Strengths and Weaknesses of the Study

There were strengths and weaknesses within this study. The first weakness was that this study was limited to female veterans who served in 2004 or later. This greatly limited the recruitment and decreased the amount of information that could have been collected if it had been opened to all female veterans or veterans who served earlier than 2004. This researcher did not achieve the intended sample size, and limiting the years of services to 2004 or later may have weakened the study. Another weakness was that a field test was not conducted due to the limited time this researcher had to complete the remainder of her book process. The field test could have assisted with identifying any problem areas before completing the data collection, analysis, and interpretation. The third weakness encompasses the limitations of mental health care examination. Mental health encompasses many different areas, and only applying these concepts to QoL and well-being omits a wealth of information that could be collected about the mental health of our veterans.

This study also provided some strengths. The first strength was obtaining information directly from the female veterans who had experienced the problem. This allowed for more in-depth descriptions utilizing open-ended and follow-up questions to obtain important information for future implications. This area provided rich details that can advance this knowledge base in the future. Another strength of this study is that this researcher is a mental health professional and was able to identify distress and guide the individual interviews in a healthy way, eliciting more details for the study.

Recommendations

In this study, I described how female veteran survivors of active-duty MST described their engagement with mental health care and its effects on their QoL and wellbeing. After completing this study and identifying the strengths and weaknesses, several recommendations for further research have been identified. This researcher has also explained the recommendations for future practice. Based on the results of this study, further research is indicated in the areas of the study population, data collection tools, and included participants.

Recommendations for Future Research

Based on the results of this study, there are several recommendations for future research:

1. The focus of this study was how female veterans of military sexual trauma have encountered mental health care after discharge and how those services affected their quality of life and or well-being. I recommend that future research focus on other aspects of mental health care, not just QoL and well-being. Mental health resources provide many different aspects of care and can provide different levels of care that are also important to understand to affect change in the future.

2. My research focused on female veterans who served in the military anytime in
2004 or afterward to account for the establishment of the Sexual Assault and Prevention Response Office. It is also important to examine and speak with our female veterans who served before 2004 to understand the care that they have or have not received and how it has affected their mental health care. The level of need for veterans who served after 2004 to those who served before 2004 may be different. An understanding of these differences would be important for future research.
3. This research focused solely on female veterans. Future research focused on male veterans who have experienced MST while enlisted and the mental health care that they have received is an important aspect of understanding the needs of our male veteran survivors of MST.

4. My collected research data included a questionnaire, individual interviews, and reflection journals. Future research that utilizes a focus group and other collection tools, such as a variety of Likert-type surveys that focus on issues surrounding sexual trauma, mental health services and the various therapies available, and a longitudinal study to assess the effect(s) of sexual trauma over time could be effective and provide information to add to the body of knowledge.

5. My study represented only three of the six military branches, which was not an equal reflection of all military branches or the services they have, are, or may provide in the future. Future research that intentionally recruits from all military branches could obtain more balanced information about this topic.

6. Before the completion of my study, it was not known how female military survivors of active-duty military sexual trauma would

describe the effects of their post-military provided mental health care services on their quality of life and well-being. This topic was limited in the literature, thus creating the problem space for my study. I addressed the problem space by understanding how female veterans of active-duty MST described the effects of the mental health care services that they received as veterans and how the care contributed to their quality of life and well-being.

Recommendations for Future Practice

I have several recommendations for future practice. The first and second recommendation for future practice is related to the implementation of new or more focused mental health care for female veteran survivors of MST. The information obtained from the research participants shared concern about wait times for care and that having a supportive, effective mental health professional was one of the most important tools for improved QoL and well-being. The need to provide effective solutions to decrease wait times to see a mental health provider could reduce the negative emotions and feelings that veterans shared about obtaining veteran care. However, the second recommendation may directly relate to the first. If the mental health system is able to hire, train, and retain more mental health providers in the area of treating veterans, then that could have a positive effect on wait time and provide more mental health providers who are sensitive to the needs of our female veterans.

Veterans and mental health professionals can benefit from reading and implementing the results of this study. Veterans can benefit because oftentimes, with mental health, isolation is inevitable. Reading this study and possibly identifying with some of the experiences of other veterans could be helpful. Also, mental health professionals and facilities that provide mental health to veterans could benefit from reading and implementing the results of this study. Understanding the ways that consumers of veteran mental health perceive the things that help or exacerbate their mental health can assist in implementing new ways of treatment to promote support in those areas. Maybe this research will inspire a mental health provider to obtain additional training or inspire veterans to continue to advocate for themselves and push for the needed care.

Holistic Reflection on the Problem Space

Although MST has existed for many years, there remains limited research that examined how mental health services contributed to the female veteran QoL and wellbeing after assault (Kelly, 2021; Kintzle et al., 2015; Matt et al., 2020; Reinhardt et al., 2023). Before I completed my study, not know was how female military survivors of active-duty military sexual trauma would describe the effects of their post-military provided mental health care services on their quality of life and well-being (Brown et al., 2021; Calhoun et al., 2018; Holland et al., 2016; Kintzle et al., 2015; Matt et al., 2020;

Starzynski et al., 2017). I addressed the problem space in this research.

Utilizing the theoretical framework from Maslow's Hierarchy of Needs and Deci and Ryan's self-determination theory 1985a), I conducted a study to identify how female veterans experienced mental health care and how it affected their quality of life and wellbeing. Three data sources were used to collect rich data: a quality of life questionnaire

(QOLS), individual semi-structured open-ended interviews, and a reflection journal. Twenty veterans completed the QOLS, 12 participated in the interviews, and one completed the reflection journal. The conclusions drawn from the data collection showed that: (a) Female veterans described long wait times as difficulties with their experiences with mental health care after discharge; (b) Female veterans described having a supportive mental health provider as a positive experience after discharge; and (c) Once engaged in the services, mental health services and support contributed to positive wellbeing and quality of life. This body of information may add to the literature and inform those caring for female veterans with MST about their needs and what is vital to this population.

www.ingramcontent.com/pod-product-compliance
Lightning Source LLC
Chambersburg PA
CBHW071344230926
51846CB00002B/440
* 9 7 8 8 1 1 8 8 8 1 4 4 5 *